DIVINE
Conversations

DIVINE
Conversations

The Art of Meaningful Dialogue with God

How to Listen & Learn,
Be Healed & Transformed

by

SIGNA BODISHBAUGH

www.wyattpublishing.com
Mobile, Alabama

Wyatt House books may be ordered through booksellers or by contacting:

WYATT HOUSE PUBLISHING
399 Lakeview Dr. W.
Mobile, Alabama 36695
www.wyattpublishing.com

Because of the dynamic nature of the Internet, any web address or links contained in this book may have changed since publication and may no longer be valid. The views expressed in this book are solely those of the author and do not necessarily reflect those of the publisher, and the publisher hereby disclaims any responsibility for them.

Interior design by: Mark Wyatt
Cover design by: Mary Ann Wyatt

ISBN 13 TP: 978-0-9882209-7-3
Library of Congress Control Number: 2013935857

Printed in the United States of America

for Coach
and
for Conlee

CONTENTS

CLARIFICATIONS

All Biblical references are from the New International Version, which is my daily study Bible, unless otherwise noted.

All references to God and The Bible are capitalized out of respect for Him, for His Word, and for clarification.

Any reference to scripture is capitalized: *The Word of God.* Any reference to personal words from God is not capitalized: *the word of God.*

I used fictitious names when writing about real events in the lives of others, either because it was not possible to obtain their permission, or because they should have the opportunity to tell their own story in first person when they are ready. Sometimes I changed a few minor circumstances to give them more anonymity but each account is accurate.

Many of my generic references to humankind use a masculine pronoun. I do this for several reasons without any excuses, without any sexist agendas, and without being exclusive. It avoids the awkwardness of using he/she for inclusivity. My generic references encompass male and female equally. Besides that, I raised three sons and tend to think that way.

INTRODUCTION

Have you ever felt a cringe or twinge inside when you heard someone say that God spoke to them? Maybe you had doubts if they said, "God told me to do that" or "God spoke to my heart about this," or "God led me to make this decision." If so, then I hope you will read every word in this book. Granted, sometimes people throw God's Name around when they try to make a point, to give more leverage to their own opinions. And granted, there are some seriously confused people out there who are under the influence of spirits that are not holy, who blaspheme the Name of God, and use Him for their own purposes.

Don't let a notorious few rob you of the most exciting and healing journey of a lifetime! You are created to be able to spend time in the intimate place of His presence where you actually discern the voice of the Lord.

I love the idea of going into an enclosed space with God just to be in His presence, like Moses and Joshua did in the Tent of Meeting in the wilderness. God designated this tent to be a place where *"I will meet with you and speak with you."*[1] He consecrat-

---

1   Exodus 29:42b

13

ed (set apart for His purposes) the place by His glory.[2] This means that His presence was so intense that it brought the atmosphere of heaven to a place on earth where earthbound humans could experience what is divine. In that glory, Moses was changed so drastically that even his outward appearance was aglow with the presence of God. He actually veiled his face when he left the tent. When I imagine such a phenomenon, I picture Moses covered in a holy light while being in God's presence. The psalmist tells us that *"He wraps Himself in light as with a garment, and stretches out the heavens like a tent."*[3]

Being in such a holy light transformed Moses in the same way Jesus was transformed on a mountain side while He was praying. Peter, James and John, who accompanied Jesus there, witnessed such a change in His appearance that they said, *"The appearance of His face changed, and His clothes became as bright as a flash of lightning."*[4] They also saw Moses and Elijah, **clothed in the same splendor**, talking with Jesus. These are the effects of divine conversations!

What did God and Moses do in that tent that caused such a change in a man? They obviously did more than just sit in the shade together, out of the desert heat. We are told that, *"The Lord would speak to Moses face to face, as a man speaks with his friend."*[5] Moses spent a lot of time alone with God, learning to recognize His voice so clearly that he never questioned who was speaking to him in the future. They must have shared dreams, desires and ideas with one another because Moses learned the

---

2   Exodus 29:43
3   Psalm 104:2
4   Luke 9:29
5   Exodus 33:11

character of God. There must have been instruction, healing, transformation, and empowerment given by God because Moses became a leader and a prophet.

Moses left the tent knowing God's voice. Moses left the tent trusting God always to do the right thing. Moses left the tent staking his life on their relationship. Moses left the tent transformed.

And all of this transformation occurred in the confines of a private place where Moses could meet regularly with God. Would you say that God transformed Moses to change the world? I would!

With all my heart, I believe that if you spend private time with God, listening and learning, He will transform your life, and use you to change your world as well. Paul teaches that, *"We, who with unveiled faces all reflect the Lord's glory, are being transformed into His likeness with ever-increasing glory, which comes from the Lord, who is the Spirit."*[6]

Knowing and trusting God, and entering into divine conversations with Him, can empower you in ways you cannot imagine. Let's explore together how we can enter into His tent and experience all of the wonders that He has planned for us!

---

6   2 Corinthians 3:18

CHAPTER 1
THE ART OF CONVERSATION

The best conversations I have with God are often in the early morning hours when my world is quiet and there are no distractions. I'm talking about 4:00 or 4:30 in the morning, - really early. I'm not sure how He does it exactly, but He will plant a little spark in my mind or imagination while I am sleeping, and then I am wide awake, up and listening. Sometimes it's an inspiration for something to write. Sometimes it's to read a certain book or scripture. Sometimes it's just to listen to what He is saying.

This morning He wanted to have a conversation with me about mushrooms and Mama. I listened, I asked questions, I wrote in my Listening Prayer Journal, and I learned a lot. But then, I always learn a lot when I settle in to hear what He says. God is a great conversationalist!

Recently I went for the first time to a large local Asian market. It was like walking into a much smaller version of China Town in San Francisco or Victoria, B.C. These are the only two China Towns I've ever been to and they were fascinating. The smells, foreign foods, cooking implements, sounds of clatter and chatter were all intriguing. I loved it!

Our local Asian market was not crowded the morning I was there, so I took a shopping cart and walked leisurely up and down every aisle, looking at everything. One of the things I came home with was a huge bag of dried Shiitake mushrooms. They were the ugliest things I've ever seen, but you got so many of them for such a small price, I couldn't resist. My first experiment with hydrating and cooking with them was just that: an experiment. This is what God wanted to talk about this morning.

He reminded me that although the Shiitakes looked inedible and actually pretty disgusting, there was a meaty goodness locked inside them, just waiting to be released. At first, I followed the instructions on the package (the small part that was in English) and soaked them for about one hour in cold water. It did little to improve their appearance although they plumped up somewhat. They were still too tough to slice with my best chef's knife. Then I heated some water and soaked them in that for a while. This, too, helped. They sliced better, but seemed more like softened cardboard than a mushroom. Then, I thought of slowly simmering them in homemade chicken stock. Oh my goodness! They were delicious! They are now my new favorite go-to ingredient.

Immediately, I saw the application God had here for me. I quickly recognized the imagery of the gradual progression of moving from a brittle, dried-up soul to coming to life in one's full potential. He's really good at making those kinds of applications from the most ordinary things.

God not only initiates great conversations, He changes subjects rapidly. But He always has a purpose and always makes a point if I stay with Him. Just when I thought this was my lesson for the morning, He got personal. *Do you remember how hard and unloving your mother always seemed to you when she was around her mother?* I did indeed remember. It was a mystery to me. My mother always called my grandmother by her first name, Bertie, with no terms of endearment or signs of affection. She "did her duty" with her mother and nothing more.

I called my grandmother "Mamo." She poured love and affirmation upon me and I soaked it up. But she and my mother behaved as strangers to one another. Even on the day Mamo died, my mother's last words to her were, "I can't forgive you."

I knew parts of their story. Bertie married an older man, a wealthy, prominent physician, when she was only sixteen. Her parents were thrilled. Within a year she was expecting their first child (my mother) and her husband insisted she have an abortion. This was in 1912, but doctors were able to do such things even then. Bertie was horrified and refused. Whatever selfish, twisted, evil intent that was in this man's heart was revealed and he walked out, abandoning his family, never to be heard from again.

Bertie moved from a lovely home with servants back to the modest home of her parents. Shame and embarrassment covered the family. Divorce was considered a stigma. A baby in the home was a constant reminder. There was no alimony or child support required by law at that time, so Bertie went to work in a jewelry store and strict, disapproving grandparents raised my mother.

The tragic actions of one self-centered man filtered down through my mother's family until he was forgotten. For some strange reason the blame for shame was transferred to my grandmother instead of being placed on her wayward husband. Perhaps it was because she was present and he was not. For whatever reason, Mamo became the scapegoat for the family.

Dysfunction can become normal in a family if that's all you've ever known. I never understood my mother's refusal to forgive my grandmother, especially when my mother was born again when she was in her sixties. But, when you live long enough with your family dynamics, you quit questioning after a while.

In the same way God changed the subject from mushrooms to Mama, He reminded me of an afternoon I was visiting my mother shortly after Mamo died. We were sitting on her front porch, drinking iced tea. Thinking she might want to remember some good things about Mamo, I casually asked, "What are some of your earliest memories about your mother?" An anger rose up in my mother I had never seen before, and I had seen her angry many times.

"I'll tell you what I remember. I remember my sixth birthday. I had a new blue hair ribbon and Bertie said she would take me to the movies. I was so excited I could hardly wait until she got home from work. But she came home with a man she worked with, and they said they were going to the movies. I thought at first I could go too, but we were standing at the corner in front of our house, waiting for the streetcar, and she told me to go on back in the house. She said I couldn't go with them. She didn't care what I wanted. She never cared what I wanted."

That one memory summed up a lifetime of my mother's disappointment and a sense of rejection. Of course, the real villain in the story was my grandfather, but he was gone and Mamo bore the brunt of my mother's sense of abandonment, not being wanted, and overwhelming covering of shame.

The Lord said to me, *Your mother thought of herself as one of those dehydrated mushrooms, no life, no flavor, and nothing of beauty.*

My heart cried out, "Oh, Lord. I wish I had known then how to minister to her. But at the time I was just learning about how You can transform lives. You were transforming me and I was still fragile. I missed so many opportunities with my mother."

And then, as He always does, He got to the point of this early morning conversation He initiated. *I wish you could see her now! She has been steeped in My love and she is the lovely one I created her to be, full of eternal life. You will see for yourself one day.*

Conversations with God Transform Lives!

I don't know why God initiated this particular conversation with me about my mother. She died in 1997, and I wasn't thinking about her or remembering a significant birth date or death date. He just thought it was something I needed to hear. The conversation was detailed, yet rather rambling. It involved several long-forgotten memories and some powerful symbols. It didn't last very long but it made a strong impact on me. It filled me with hope, love, redemption, anticipation, joy, and deep gratitude. It was surprising and it came unexpectedly.

There are other times when a conversation with God is very succinct and powerfully hits the mark without any preamble, symbolism or explanations. He just speaks a word or a few words and a life can be transformed. I remember Brenda, a woman we have known for several years. She first came to us with her life in shambles. She struggled with broken relationships, addictions, self-inflicted wounds, self-hatred, and very little trust in God. Over and over we and others would tell her that the One who was her only Helper was the very One she was turning away from. She wanted help but she didn't want Him.

When she was a child, Brenda had been abused in a church by one of the elders. Her immature mind rationalized that it was in God's house and therefore, He allowed it to happen. From that time on she turned her back on Him. When we met her she was desperate and suicidal.

Conlee and I spent hours and hours with her over the next several years, loving, encouraging, exhorting, preaching, quoting scripture, and eventually, becoming frustrated. We were only two people of many who tried to help Brenda. Each of us did all we knew to do and she continued to sink lower. Occasionally she would rally slightly but her general decline was steady. Eventually she was no longer able to work and received medical disability.

One day, after several weeks, we saw Brenda and she looked like a different person. Everything was different about her: her countenance, her mannerisms, her attitude, even her posture. We couldn't wait to find out what happened. She said that in a moment of utter despair she found herself crying out to God, complaining once again and feeling sorry for herself. He spoke to her in an unmistakable way and it transformed her almost immediately.

What he said to her was not at all what I would have told her, or what I thought she needed to hear. It was certainly not anything I expected God to say. I'm not sure how I would have reacted if He had said it to me. But, as always, His words were perfectly suited for the person they were intended for. They were perfect for Brenda.

Here's what she heard. *Brenda, it's not all about you. It's all about Me.*

That was it. Those words hit the mark. They were like lightening striking within her. And it was the beginning of a restored and healed life that is continuing to bear fruit for Him.

Trusting Your Conversation Partner

The conversation I had with God about mushrooms and Mama came so unexpectedly, so effortlessly and in such detail, that it might seem to you that you can't relate. Let me assure you that I didn't begin to hear God this easily overnight. It took desire, priority, and practice.

In a mysteriously wonderful way, God enables each of His creatures to respond to Him. The heavens (the skies, sun, moon, stars, planets, and galaxies) declare His glory.[7] The beasts are endowed by Him with instincts that allow them to relate to their environments in amazing ways.[8] But we, the crown of all of His creation, are given not only the ability to declare His glory through our lives, and to reflect His brilliance through the instincts He places within us,[9] we, also, are given a human spirit that comes alive by His Holy Spirit. This uniquely enables us to hear His voice in a very personal way and to be in relationship with Him.

I can refuse to listen, choose to do other things, or even decide He has nothing to say to me. Whatever I believe makes

---

7   Psalm 19:1

8   Job 12:7

9   For instance, we take for granted that a newborn baby knows to suck in order to receive nourishment.

no difference about what God does; it only affects what I receive. God's word is constantly going forth, creating, restoring, transforming. When I choose to put myself in the best position possible to hear what God is saying to me, I am always enlightened, often surprised, and never disappointed. Every time I hear His voice I am changed. Sometimes in large and powerful ways, sometimes in smaller, endearing, tender ways. It is always important.

Initially, to even have the desire to hear what He wanted to say to me, I had to work on the trust factor in our relationship. I didn't grow up knowing Jesus as my Savior and my best friend. His presence first became a major part of my life when I was a young adult, and at first I wasn't sure if I wanted to reveal to Him my deepest thoughts and needs. Trust takes time.[10] Lovingly, He gave me the gift of time and offered every opportunity for me to get to know Him in ways I never thought possible.

It's sort of a *Catch-22*[11] situation for me. I need to spend time with Him in order to trust Him more, but at the same time I need to trust Him more to have the desire to spend more time with Him. But, for God, this isn't a *Catch-22* at all. He interrupts our circular thinking and infuses us with deeper trust in ways we cannot begin to expect or imagine. All we have to do is say, "Help! Teach me!"

Conversation is an art, which means it is motivated by creativity. God, the Creator, is also the Great Conversationalist. First of all, He always listens. Then, when He speaks, His words

---

10   After Brenda's transformation, it became apparent that God had been revealing Himself to her little by little over the months of her resistance. One of the ways He did this was through many people continuing to pour His love into her, even when she did not seem to receive it.

11   The term "Catch-22," taken from the title of the novel by Joseph Heller, implies a way of circular thinking that brings one through a series of thought processes to solve a problem back to the original problem itself.

can turn any of us from desiccated mushrooms into exquisite delicacies. His example of initiating, motivating, and sustaining conversations with His children is one we should seek and practice. Without the joys of divine conversations we miss many opportunities to come closer to His heart and to be transformed by His love.

Good conversation, both with God and with others, has a flow and a rhythm that moves somewhere. Conversation can be planned or can erupt spontaneously. Some of us had good childhood examples and experiences of meaningful conversation, and we easily adapted to it at an early age. This greatly enhances one's ability to speak with God.

But others of us have been stifled or deprived of conversation partners, and we need to be taught how to converse effectively and how to practice.

Unfortunately, there are also those who just give up and remain detached from one of the most significantly life-changing experiences God offers us. My opinion is that we make it much too difficult. What should be an innate part of being God's beloved child, instead becomes a chore or a task we find too draining or too tedious.

> *Good conversation is composed of two equal components:*
> ***listening** and **speaking**.*
> *Participants in genuine conversation share*
> ***common interests, familiarity**, and **trust**.*
> *The **fruit** of genuine conversation is that the*
> *participants move into*
> *an ever-increasingly, ever-deepening, close heart relationship.*

Sometimes even strangers can find themselves in stimulating conversations with one another simply because they are focused on an interest common to all involved. Have you ever listened to fishermen around the bait shop discussing what kind of fish are biting? Or women in the beauty shop sharing stories about their children? Or customers in the check-out line comparing prices about a certain food item? However, their common interests alone do not promote a closeness that will necessarily lead to or sustain a relationship. Such casual conversationalists may not even know each other's names or anything personal about one another. **Common interest alone is not enough for conversation to bear fruit.**

Members of the same family may regularly converse about trivial matters. *What time will you be home? Who is going to pick up the children? We have a ball game tonight.* Although information is exchanged, matters of the heart are ignored. **Familiarity alone is not enough for conversation to bear fruit.**

When both common interests and familiarity are present in a relationship, the opportunity for genuine conversation is much easier. However, in a divine conversation, another vital ingredient is trust. When we trust God, we are willing to be vulnerable with Him, to have an open heart, and to let down our defenses. When the element of trust is present, we can enjoy the full potential: a closeness or intimacy with Him on a much deeper level.

This priceless combination (*common interest, familiarity,* and *trust*) enhances any relationship: a friendship, a marriage, and especially, your relationship with God.

This art form of conversation comes very naturally to some people. It is a joy to observe the natural tendency in some men and women who have no guile, no reluctance at all to be honest and genuine in their relationships. Without any posturing or discomfort, they are invitational to the rest of us to join in with their easy ways of relating to themselves, to God and to others. Their openness calls forth a desire in others to be more genuine.

However, that desire may seem impossible to achieve for people who are filled with self-consciousness, shyness and fear. Any conversation other than the most trivial may be difficult and even painful. The thought of being vulnerable to another person, even to God, may be enough to cause them to retreat into themselves.

Obstacles to Conversation

There are many obstacles to the art of meaningful conversation. Sometimes just by identifying the hindrances, by realizing we are not alone in our struggles and that there is help for us, we can be encouraged. Here are just a few common obstacles.

- **Poor Family Examples**

Much of what we pick up about conversing we learn in our childhood home. Lots of factors are involved. If you had a very verbal older sibling, you probably didn't need to talk much; someone expressed your needs and opinions for you.

If you grew up in a tense family environment, perhaps no one listened to one another because each one was so wrapped up in personal problems. In such a situation you internalize very quickly the idea that no one cares what you think, and so you keep your thoughts locked up within.

If all conversation in your family went through one person,

you may have been denied a voice. A problem person in the family will dominate this role, and others will defer to him/her to avoid conflict. A "problem person" in a family is not necessarily one living in sin. Yes, it can be an alcoholic or other addict, one whose anger knows no bounds, or one who is very self-centered and demanding. But a person with special needs can also consume a family's attention to the extent that other family members have no voice in matters that are not centered on the one with the most needs.

If your family only gathered for meals around the television, you never got the opportunity to practice the art of conversing at table. Because of the infrequency of family conversation, your only memories may be of stressful holidays, forced niceness, or painful arguments among family members.

Being at a table with family and friends is a natural venue for practicing the art of conversation. I was denied this opportunity when I was young. As the only child in the family I was told to sit quietly, put my napkin in my lap, chew with my mouth closed, try a bite of everything, and keep silent. I mostly listened to my parents argue. I was never asked for my opinion or invited to share anything I was interested in. As a result, when I became old enough to join in conversations with friends, I was self-conscious about what I would say and how they would react to my opinions. I assumed they didn't want to hear what I thought about anything and I assumed I would be ignored. Conversation was not a natural activity for me at all. In fact, it was often painful. It took me many years to discover the source of these confusing tendencies. Only by learning to have genuine conversation with God was this early childhood implant removed from my soul.

Aware that sometimes others who sit around our dining

room table today may have struggled with the same kind of deprivations, I often make it a point to ask non-threatening questions to our guests, drawing each one into the circle of conversation. The key to doing this effectively is then to really listen to what they say. Nothing inhibits quality conversation like asking someone his opinion and then looking away, acting disinterested, or ignoring what he says. Follow-up responses are just as important as initial volleys in conversation.

- **Modern Techno-Gadgets**

Quality conversations are severely limited by today's common practice of texting. This is a particular pet peeve of mine! Have you ever attempted to talk with someone who won't look up from the cell phone in his hand? He will assure you that he hears every word you say, but it is obvious you do not have his full attention. The same person who will defend texting anywhere, anytime, would probably consider it rude to pick up a newspaper and begin to read it while talking to you. In my opinion, there is little difference.

A few years ago I was with my husband at the home of a young single mom. Her refrigerator was broken and Conlee was fixing it for her so she wouldn't have to call a repair service. He was behind the refrigerator, working, and she was standing right in front of it. He was talking to her about the problem and asking her questions. The whole time I watched her absorbed in her cell phone, texting and smiling. She didn't hear a word he said.

One of our sons, a building contractor, says he has to tell his employees NOT to use cell phones for texting while meeting with clients. The younger employees argue that they can successfully text, even under the conference table, and keep their full attention on what the client is saying. But it is just a fact that unless you also are texting, you will feel slighted and ignored by those around you.

Eye contact and full attention are vital to engaging in authentic conversation. When we desire to hear from God and intentionally begin to practice, we will find that keeping our full attention and the eyes of our heart on Him rather than on many other distractions will be our hardest challenge, and one we tend to rationalize. It is something we all have to work on and submit to. Rather than defending our position of what is important and what we can juggle (like texting while conversing) we will learn from Him how to focus and engage with Him whole-heartedly.

- **Noise Pollution**

Texting is just one of the many modern obstacles to the art of conversation. Noise is another one. Where can you go today where you are surrounded by quiet? Even alone in the car most people turn on the radio or a CD. One of our granddaughters said the mother who drove her car pool every morning always put on the same DVD for the kids to watch on the way to school. No one ever talked and they watched the same fifteen minutes of a movie for nine months.

Enjoying the beach with the soothing sound of the waves crashing on the surf can be interrupted by the loud music of people who set up their boom boxes nearby. We are forced to listen to music while shopping and riding elevators. Does silence make people that uncomfortable? Many people walk around with ear buds firmly attached, listening to something all the time. I recently looked at some pictures of a young friend visiting Europe for the first time. In every picture, in front of every place of interest, he had his ear buds attached and wires connecting him to something else.

We have been through several hurricanes and tropical storms here on the Gulf Coast when power lines were blown down. One of the most amazing experiences in the aftermath of each one is the absolute quiet when all the power is off. At first the total silence is unnerving. There is no familiar gentle hum of electrical appliances, air blowing through AC vents, or background music. All of those things that we are accustomed to hearing, which form a "white noise" in our lives, are gone. Just silence. Of course, it doesn't take long for generators to get cranked up and chain saws to blast out, but for a few hours we experience pure silence. It takes such a marked absence of sounds to make one realize how surrounded we are by noise all the time.

• **Attention Deficit**

My husband, Conlee, always says that people will open up to me about the most personal things, even more than to a pastor or a therapist. It's true that I ask questions, but mostly I listen. Because of this, I often run into people who immediately begin to share some of the most intimate details of their life.

Most recently, my daughter-in-law, Margo, and I were making a last minute pre-Thanksgiving run to the grocery store. While she was placing our items on the conveyor belt, I became engaged in a conversation with the man behind me who had an adorable baby daughter in his cart. Just by asking about her, and listening, he proceeded to show me a picture on his phone of his baby's cells fertilized in a petri dish as a result of in vitro fertilization. I learned how long it took, how many cells fertilized, and how excited he was to have a child. As we walked to the car, Margo said, "Only you, Signa, get people to tell you their most intimate details." It only happened because I asked him questions about his baby and then really listened.

This seems natural to me now. But that wasn't always the case. I had to learn how to be open to genuine conversation. It didn't come from my childhood background; conversation was woefully lacking there. It didn't come from any psychological training; I haven't had any. It didn't come from reading copious books about how to develop the art of conversation; I haven't read any. It came primarily from wanting to converse with God. He taught me how to listen. When we learn to hear His voice, it is so much easier to truly hear one another.

An important, large part of good conversation (with God or anyone) is genuine listening. But when you begin to think about this seriously, you realize how far short we all come. A lot of conversation is reduced to half listening and half mentally preparing what you will say next. Or it's half listening and half looking for an opportunity to move on. Perhaps the times when people open their hearts to share with me it's because these are the times I am trying to give them my full attention in the present moment and asking them questions about what they are talking about. This isn't always easy because of the many distractions all around us. Blocking out other conversations, random thoughts, and pressing needs demands my intentional concentration and purpose.

This kind of personal attention even in the most mundane situations has amazing results. When a checker hands me my receipt with a casual, "Have a good day!" as I leave a store, I almost always try to look that person in the eye and genuinely receive the blessing. I know they may be trained by a manager to say the same thing to every customer, but when I listen and respond,

"You have a really good day, too!" I mean it, and they usually hear it, often surprised. Several years ago I made the decision to both receive such a comment and return it as a form of a blessing. It's amazing how that same checker remembers me the next time and is especially friendly, perhaps even wants to talk.

• Meaningless Chit-Chat

A lot of what we tend to call conversation is really just an exchange of chit-chat. Whether I know someone well or not, I am just not good at this kind of small talk. I never have been. I hate what is sometimes called "cocktail party conversation." Because I'm not good at it, I find it really boring. For instance, I've never been one to talk endlessly on the phone. In fact, I'm often amazed at people who are pushing a grocery cart with one hand and talking on their cell phone with the other. (They always hold up the flow in the aisles when they do this, too!) Most of the conversations you overhear as you walk by sound totally unnecessary and meaningless. In fact, it usually sounds more like gossip and just a way to stay connected with someone while shopping rather than like genuine conversation.

Talking just to be talking is not conversation. Talking just to pass the time is not conversation. Talking because you are bored is not conversation. Talking just to fill empty "air time" is not conversation. I know a couple of people who will begin to speak and then do not seem to know how to stop until they are interrupted. (I've heard some people pray this way, too).

People with a "gift for gab" may not be very adept in conversation at all. They may be great in crowds to "break the ice," or to make shy people feel more comfortable. But they may not be able to curb their desire to keep speaking long enough to really listen to someone else. When you leave out the vital component of listening, the potential for genuine conversation (intimacy and a deeper heart connection) is ignored and unmet.

There are lots of reasons why many people never achieve genuine conversation.

What are some of your roadblocks?

The Art of Conversation Can Be Learned!

If I am going to have a conversation with anyone, I want it to have some kind of genuine content: either to be interesting, challenging, fun, informative, stimulating, enlightening, or conveying heart emotions. Obviously, I am not talking about business conversations, exchanges of information, or conversations with strangers here. I'm referring to one friend conversing with another friend because they care about one another.

It's fun to use a little creativity to practice this art form. Something our children and grandchildren like to do is have "Silver Bowl Night." This is when we stay at table after the meal and pass around a silver bowl filled with questions. Each one draws a question, reads it aloud, answers it and then asks someone else at the table to answer it as well. The questions are open-ended ones, like: *What is the best dessert you've ever eaten? Where would you go on vacation if money was no object? What was the funniest trick someone ever played on you?*

This is always a fun time for everyone, even for those who

are the most shy. Our adult children almost always groan when The Silver Bowl appears, but they quickly get into it because it is fascinating to discover how much you can learn about a person you thought you knew! And it all starts by asking questions, listening and responding.

Reading and honestly discussing a book (especially The Bible) together can develop the art of conversation. It involves the exchange of ideas and opinions, observations and experiences.

Argument stifles authentic conversation.

Taking a class with someone and sharing with one another what you are learning, what you are struggling with, and how you are applying your new knowledge can develop conversation.

Forcing your opinions on another person or belittling opposing ideas will inhibit a conversation.

Joining a club where you share a common goal with others can stimulate conversation.

Watching TV and playing electronic games are pretty much conversation-killers.

> *What are activities you enjoy with others that*
> *stimulate good conversation?*
> *What activities inhibit it?*

Is it any wonder that we have difficulty hearing God? I know God can do anything, even interrupt our preoccupation with self, our constant noise, and our endless distractions. But most often, **He invites us to tune in to the way He wants to converse.** He invites us into His tent.

For most of us, that is not easy. We have to work at it. We

have to learn new skills - skills we have forgotten, skills that aren't very popular any more, skills that take deliberation, concentration, and time. But it can be done! And it can be so much fun! Not only will learning these new skills enhance every human relationship (and even heal some fractured ones!), you will find the joy of an ever increasing, intimate fellowship with your Lord Jesus Christ. In His own words:

"If anyone hears My voice and opens the door, I will come in and eat with him, and he with Me."
(Rev. 3:20)

CHAPTER 2
PRIORITIES AND PROBLEMS

It's helpful to appreciate the principles for general conversations in order to have the most effective conversations with a holy God. When you enter into divine conversations with Him you will be learning to share your heart, listen with interest and expectation to what He says, ask questions, listen some more, and respond. Even if you have never been comfortable with conversation before, He wants to teach you. He will help you overcome all your inadequacies and your misunderstandings. He longs to be close to you!

THE RHYTHM OF GOOD CONVERSATION
Share. Listen. Respond. Ask. Listen. Respond. Ask. Listen. Respond. Ask. Listen. Respond. Ask.

This is the same rhythm you learn to converse effectively with men and women, yet with God there is an incredible added dimension: His words to you will go deep into your soul and change your life. You will know Him more intimately and in knowing Him, your life will change more and more into the person He created you to be.

When I teach anywhere, I like to begin with this group prayer. When I begin to read the Bible, I pray it. When I begin to write, I pray it. It is deceptively simple, yet powerful.

Lord Jesus,
Speak to my heart.
Change my life.
And make me whole.
Amen.

Here's what this prayer means to me:

- *Speak to my heart*: I believe that God speaks to me. I anticipate what He says. I listen for His words. I know His words bring life and wholeness to me. He is the Living Word. He is in me.

- *Change my life*: Whenever His word enters into me, He is changing me more and more into His image. His words do in me what no human wisdom can. He knows my heart better than I do. He wants what is best for me.

- *And make me whole*: When God changes me it is always towards wholeness. He wants me to be whole more than I do.

Pray this prayer out loud, thinking deliberately
about what you are asking of Him!

Praying about, thinking about, talking about, and writing about hearing God's voice provokes some interesting and often surprisingly vivid memories. When God brings our memories to the forefront, He uses them for His healing purposes, to make us whole. Even as I wrote out the simple prayer above, I began to wonder: *When was the first time I ever thought about hearing God speak to me?* And then a memory flooded in with amazing details.

Sometimes God prompts me to flow with the initial memories that pop up, to see where they lead, even though they seem insignificant. This particular memory really surprised me, and in it God revealed the root source of a deep-seated but hidden fear I had when I was young. His love enabled me to overcome that fear as I began to know Him intimately when I was born again at age thirty-two. But I never understood why it had impacted me in such a paralyzing way for so many years. Hearing His voice just recently through this memory brought revelation and understanding, and with it an even deeper closeness and love for Him. It is an example of hearing His voice in an unexpected way and being drawn closer into His heart.

Here is the memory that came back so vividly as I wrote it in my Journal. You can see that some of the details appear to be totally irrelevant; however, it is helpful to write them all out because they keep you on track to get to the goal God has in mind. I emboldened the part I knew He was highlighting for me.

I was ten years old and it was my birthday. Lying in bed that night I was still excited about my "town-sweep" skating party where I was showered with dozens of presents, including a puppy given to me by a boy named Bob

Broccoli. Bob had gotten the puppy for free from the animal shelter. My mother didn't know this or she would have taken him back that very day. She didn't like dogs very much and at first said, "No way!" But later she had to admit that he was "as cute as a button." So, his name became Bobby Buttons.

Bobby Buttons was curled up asleep on the floor next to my bed in a make-shift dog bed fashioned from a cardboard box. Beside me were spread out all the books I had received at my party. I was trying to decide which one I wanted to read first. After looking at some new Nancy Drew mysteries, a set of *Little House on the Prairie*, some Louisa May Alcott, and *Rebecca of Sunnybrook Farm* (all of which I still have), I settled on a book I had never thought of reading: The Holy Bible. It was a present from my maternal grandmother, Mamo.

Mamo and the women on her side of the family usually gave me Christmas and birthday presents that were sterling silver with my name or initials engraved on them. They believed that girls should start their hope chests at an early age. A Bible was not something I expected from her – or anyone else. We were not a religious family, seldom went to church, and to my knowledge, this was the first Bible in our home. I had never seen one in Mamo's home either. This book was covered in stiff black leather, and in the lower right of the front cover, true to Mamo's style of believing in monograms, my full name was engraved in shiny gold lettering. Even the edges of the pages were bright gold. I was almost afraid to open it.

The first page told me that it was "The King James

Version" and it had a few colored pictures scattered throughout the pages. Between the Old Testament and the New Testament were some beautifully illustrated pages for filling in the blanks for the Records of Holy Matrimony, Births, and Deaths. As a ten year old, I lay there in my bed wondering if I would ever fill out those pages, if I would ever marry, what my husband's name would be, would anyone I knew and loved die soon......

Randomly, I leafed through the pages immediately after the Records. And I remember this as if it just happened: the first verse I actually read in the Bible was Matthew 24:4-5. It was in red letters so I assumed that made it more important. *"Take heed that no man deceive you. For many shall come in my name, saying, I am Christ; and shall deceive you."*

Forgotten were Nancy Drew, Louisa May Alcott, and even Bobby Buttons. All I could picture were rows of identical bearded men, all dressed in white robes, saying over and over, "I am Christ, I am Christ, I am Christ...." And I saw myself standing in front of them, having one chance to choose which one was the real Jesus. ***How could I not be deceived? How could anyone know which one was real? They all look alike! They all sound alike! I can't trust any of them! This isn't fair!***

I closed my Bible carefully, got out of bed and put it in the very back of the bottom drawer of my dresser. Covered by my summer play clothes which I would not get out for months, it was out of sight and out of mind. In fact, I did not open that Bible, or any Bible, again for many years.

I have not accessed that memory in decades. It came suddenly when I prayed, *Speak to my heart.* I believe God was showing me something important, a turning point or cross-roads in my life, something that disconnected me from knowing Jesus and His divine conversations for many years.

Everything I Know About Conversing With God I Learned as a Child

There must be dozens of books out there in the "Everything I Know about _____, I Learned from _____" category. After years of observing our chickens, Conlee and I have even thought we could write a book titled, "Everything I Know about Life, I Learned from Chickens." Their behavior and interactions with one another teach a lot about human nature and explain many of the common expressions we often use, such as "mad as an old wet hen," "hen-pecked," "pecking order," "cock of the walk," etc. But, I digress. You get the picture!

So, in spite of my first sad biblical experience at age ten, I still think it's helpful to observe the natural behavior of children to see some of the characteristics of an avid God-conversationalist. We can learn a lot. After all, Jesus said to come to Him like a little child. There must be a reason!

In children:
- There is an openness
- There is a trust level
- There is an expectation
- There is an innocence
- There is a love of repetition of favorite things

- There is a desire to learn and grow
- There is a need for exhortation and discipline
- There is a delight in exploration and discovery

Maybe one of the reasons why this analogy works so well is that many children actually do hear God's voice very easily. We have heard so many parents say that their toddlers who are barely verbal will speak truths about God that only He could have related to them. Some little ones see angels. Some have an intense awareness of His presence. Some see the glories of Heaven. Because I have no memory (or family stories) of experiencing this as a child, I doubted the veracity of such claims. But our third son, Ben, changed my mind.

When we were born again, we already had two sons, Rick, who was nine, and Matt, who was seven. But then, five years after our new birth, God gave us our third son, Ben. From his conception, he was saturated in spiritual conversations, prayers, activities and blessings. It is not surprising that he developed an eager God-awareness.

For instance, Ben saw angels regularly when he was young. As soon as he was verbal, he would tell us very emphatically that the pictures of little naked babies with their little wings, "are **not** angels. Angels are **big!**" He would spread his little arms as wide as possible to describe what he was seeing in the Spirit realm. When confronted with pictures of beautiful, feminine-looking angels with delicate features, he always insisted that real angels did not look like that.

Ben's early God-awareness also enabled him to hear what God was saying when others were distracted. One particular day, when he was about three years old, he shared something that brought me to tears. He told me that God spoke to him often, especially when we were at our little lake cabin. This was a place about an hour from our home where we went often with the children and friends. It previously belonged to an older couple who hosted Federation of Christian Athletes' retreats there, and we often had prayer retreats and Bible study there as well. It was quiet, tranquil, isolated, and was a place that had been saturated in prayer since it was built.

I asked Ben to tell me what He heard God say to him when we were at the lake cabin. His reply was, "He says Jesus loves me."

I said, "Ben, I believe you, but I don't hear Him speak to me that often, even at the lake." He then got that adorable three-year-old indignant look on his face and said, "Mommie, He speaks to you all the time, but you don't listen!"

Out of the mouths of babes.......

It doesn't take long for the world and its values to get hold of us and ring louder in our ears than God's voice does. Soon Ben forgot to listen to God because he watched TV or became involved with a toy or was told to do something to help or had to go somewhere with the family – or whatever. This is the picture of each one of us. Even though we as parents affirmed and encouraged Ben to listen to God and to converse with Him, "stuff" and "life" got in the way and he quit listening, expecting, delighting, and discovering. He grew up into the ways of the world.

I did the same thing. At my first remembered experience of God-consciousness on my tenth birthday, I let a road-block detour my journey for many years. I've thought: *What if I had asked God how to know who the real Jesus is? What if I had al-*

lowed Him to speak to me that night? But, as my dear husband often says, "You don't play 'what if' games with God. You start right where you are!" That is wisdom. I could go down countless rabbit trails, striving to figure out all the "what-if's" in my life. What I needed most (and what we all need) is the help to find my way back to the exquisite position of hearing God's voice and responding to what He says.

It's not impossible! Many have done it and have delighted in discovering a deeper intimacy with God through meaningful conversation. Over time, I have learned to hear Him, to discern His voice from all those other voices, and to grow in deeper intimacy with Him every day. And I know, if that is your desire, you will as well. However, there are obstacles in our way. Don't be intimidated by them, just be aware and avoid them or overcome them.

CHAPTER 3
OBSTACLES

OBSTACLE #1:
YOU'RE NOT IN THE GARDEN ANYMORE

When Adam and Eve were sin-free and enjoying intimate companionship with God in the Garden, it was easy to hear His voice and it was natural. He made them that way. They were saturated with His unfiltered presence of glory all the time. But you and I do not live breath by breath in the same atmosphere of glory they once did. Because of their fall, we receive their legacy of a residue of sin in us that makes the life-style that was once so natural in the Garden now unnatural to us. For us to be acutely aware of the presence of God and to hear His voice, we enter into a supernatural way of life. This is not supernatural in the sense of what we might think of as paranormal, bizarre, or spooky. Living with God in a supernatural realm means that He lifts us *above* (super) what is natural. He removes the restrictions that limit our natural capabilities as sinful creatures. This is only possible be-cause of the sacrifice of Jesus on the cross, dying as the eternal

45

substitute for our sins. When we take His presence into our being (new birth) we are no longer bound by the restrictions of sin. We are lifted above them by the Spirit of God.

When we are born again of the Spirit, we are given the ability to live in an atmosphere where we can hear God on a regular basis as part of our intimate relationship with Him. This is what happens when we are indwelt by His Spirit.

Oh, I am aware that some people who are spiritually dead are awakened by the voice of God that penetrates their unbelief. God can supersede any barrier by walking right through it. He can walk into an unbelieving heart as well as walk through a closed door. God is God! He will do what it takes to get one's attention. But most usually He invites us to participate in the relationship; He doesn't want to monopolize it.

We hear in the Spirit realm as well as the natural realm. If Christ lives in your spirit, you dwell in the Spirit realm. It is possible to hear Him. In fact, you are able to hear Him right now. But because you don't live in the Garden, it does not come naturally. You need to intentionally practice living in the atmosphere of heaven – the presence of God. You need to tune in to His frequency rather than the ones you are accustomed to hearing.

Perhaps this is part of what God meant when He told Adam, *"By the sweat of your brow you will eat your food until you return to the ground . . ."* (Genesis 3:19a). Where once Adam had all the food he needed provided for him, after the fall he had to diligently make an effort to have food. I don't know if there were silver platters in the Garden, but for sure nothing was handed to him on one outside the Garden. For evermore Adam and his descendants would have to intentionally desire and diligently work to experience what was once given freely. In the same way, we now have to intentionally desire and make an effort to hear God's voice on a regular basis. Just as we need food for the body, we need God's word for the spirit.

There are several ways you can approach the idea of practicing (or working) to hear God's voice. One attitude might be: "Oh, no! This is just one more to-do thing I have to put on my list every day. I don't have time to take on anything else." I totally understand. This is a legitimate excuse and many of us use it. We *do* take on way too much stuff in our lives – even God stuff. We followers of Jesus often feel that every day we must do most of the following:

read the Bible/ study the Bible/ do a daily devotional/
pray for our family/pray with our family/
pray for those in need/ meet with a small group/
read a Christian book/_____

It's exhausting just listing this. And yet, there's even more – every day.

It's no wonder our initial reaction to taking on something new on a daily basis is so unappealing. How often I hear men and women say, "I just can't take on one more thing! I'm already on overload."

Time seems to be The Huge Looming Obstacle. Oh, if we could just take an "instant listening pill" or get a "divine de-coder ring!"

Some great advice I heard many years ago is this: Sometimes you have to say NO to some really good things in order to say YES to the very best.

> *What is presently on your daily routine of things to do?*
> *Write them out so you can see what you are doing*
> *(or what you're feeling guilty about not doing!)*

OBSTACLE #2:
CROSSING OFF ITEMS ON YOUR TO-DO LIST

Besides the idea that in order to be a good Christian we need to cram so many obligations into each day, many of us can become driven to perform any given task with such a rigorous, even militaristic approach, that it sucks the life out of it. An example that comes to mind (and one that was extremely helpful to show me where I might be doing the same thing) happened at a week-end house party on the Mississippi coast with several couples. We were staying in a large old family home that belonged to some dear friends. We had gathered to renew the wedding vows of our friends on their twenty-fifth anniversary. We joined four other couples, who came from various places, to spend a long week-end together and celebrate the occasion. All of us were committed Christians and we delighted in praying, talking about the Lord, and having fun together. The first morning we all gathered on the big screened porch overlooking the Gulf to have chicory coffee and beignets. One of the women had her Bible in her lap, looking down at the pages from time to time while she also engaged in the animated conversation of the group. After a while I asked her if she had a scripture she wanted to share with us. Her reply is one I will never forget.

"No, I just promised the Lord I would read a chapter a day out of the Bible and I have to get it in no matter what else is going on. Just keep talking; I'll be through in a minute."

I will admit that my initial reaction to her statement was very critical although I didn't verbally respond. But almost immediately I was struck in the heart by how often I approach God the same way. *I promised...., I should...., I am obligated...., I need to....,* - whatever. The task and goal can so easily become more important than the Person.

> *Do you have a relationship with anyone who*
> *treats you as an obligation?*
> *Do you feel reduced to someone to be*
> *catered to, checked on, or grudgingly served?*
> *How does this make you feel about that person?*
> *How does it make you feel about yourself?*

OBSTACLE #3:
PARALYZING PASSIVITY

Another attitude we can easily assume when we contemplate hearing God's voice is being passive. This is when I might say, "If God wants to speak to me, I'd love to hear what He's saying and I'll be grateful." But then I do nothing to prepare myself for listening. It's like saying I want my hair to look nice but I won't comb it or style it. Or like wanting to eat a nice home-cooked meal but I won't prepare it. Or like wanting to have a good friend but never initiating a conversation.

Passivity is a killer. It paralyzes us from enjoying life in its fullest. It diminishes the awe, wonder and potential of each opportunity. It stifles anticipation and expectation. It even prevents us from receiving incredible blessings when God opens the windows of Heaven. But passivity (along with its cousins, complacency and sloth) can be conquered!

At a recent *Journey to Wholeness*[12] conference we led, we put posters on all the doors leading into the church sanctuary where we would be meeting. In large red letters, they read: NO PASSIVITY ZONE. Each sign showed the circle with the universal symbol of NO inside by the slanted line running through it. We also projected this on the overhead screens at the beginning of the service. Without saying a word, this made people profoundly aware of how they frequently approach a worship service or a conference with the attitude of *Ok, I'm here; teach me something I haven't heard before; entertain me; pour what you've got into me, etc.* Sometimes when we begin our conferences there are even a few people sitting in the congregation with their arms crossed over their chests, as if to say *I dare you to reach me!* This time we brought it to the light. No more ignoring a common attitude. Name it! Face it! Step out of it!

Passivity has become a way of life for many – a bad habit, perhaps evidence of an unholy spirit. You may not even realize how passive you are until someone lovingly points it out to you. My favorite definition for passivity comes from the Noah Webster *1828 American Dictionary of the English Language*. It was written when our nation still had a God-consciousness in our vocabulary.

---

12   *The Journey to Wholeness in Christ* conferences led by Conlee and Signa Bodishbaugh. www.JTWIC.org

Passivity: The tendency of a body to persevere in a given state, either of motion or rest, till disturbed by another body.

Here's what I picture when I read that definition: I imagine myself wallowing in sloth, doing nothing – or the other extreme of passivity, being stuck in activism – unable to move out of either position until I am disturbed by an outside force. Notice that in Webster's definition of passivity, constant motion can keep us stuck in a given state just as much as doing nothing. We tend to think that if we are busy we are not passive, but perhaps activism as much as anything is a deterrent to living more fully in the presence of God.

I frequently ask Holy Spirit to be that "disturbance" in my life. I want Him to jolt me out of my passivity and energize me to hear what God is saying and to do what God is doing. Anytime I ask for this, almost immediately I hear God's invitation to converse with Him in a meaningful way.

Conversation is what enhanced the intimacy between God and Adam and Eve in the Garden.

Conversation with God was the hallmark of every prophet who proclaimed His will to all people.

Conversation with God was the priority for Jesus.

Conversation with Jesus and with the Father set apart the disciples, Paul, and countless saints through the ages.

And it is conversation with God that impacts us when we come out of our sloth or activism and tune into His frequency.

Divine conversation may be considered "disturbing" but it is a disturbance we desperately need.

In 1577, Sir Francis Drake, the English sea captain who circumnavigated the world, penned this prayer:

Disturb us, Lord, when
We are too well pleased with ourselves,
When our dreams have come true
Because we have dreamed too little,
When we arrived safely
Because we sailed too close to the shore.

Disturb us, Lord, when
With the abundance of things we possess
We have lost our thirst
For the waters of life;
Having fallen in love with life,
We have ceased to dream of eternity
And in our efforts to build a new earth,
We have allowed our vision
Of the new Heaven to dim.

Disturb us, Lord, to dare more boldly,
To venture on wider seas
Where storms will show your mastery;
Where losing sight of land,
We shall find the stars.
We ask You to push back
The horizons of our hopes;
And to push into the future
In strength, courage, hope and love.

> *How would you apply this poem to your own life?*
> *Are you willing to be "disturbed?"*
> *Who will you give permission to disturb you?*
> *Begin now!*

The conference where we stressed "No Passivity" was remarkably different from any other conference we ever led. Almost immediately people came forward expecting miracles. With a little encouragement, they got out of their seats; they left their comfort zones. They asked God to open the windows of Heaven and they walked *physically* as well as *spiritually* into His Glory. Healings occurred. Miracles happened. A woman with Hepatitis C was healed. A man with a serious heart problem was healed. Deaf ears were unstopped. People heard directions from the Lord. Many in bondages were set free. Why? Because, in giving God permission to speak into our lives, allowing Him to disturb us, we let down our defenses and receive the very things He wants to give us all the time. I cannot stress this enough: passivity paralyzes.

OBSTACLE #4:
THAT'S NOT MY GIFT

This is a big excuse often used to rationalize not listening to God. *Some people just don't hear God and I'm one of them.* But Jesus said, *"He who belongs to God hears what God says. The reason you do not hear is that you do not belong to God."* (John 8:47)

I trust that if you are reading this book you have a desire to hear God, and that desire comes from belonging to Him. If you belong to Him (born again) that means you *can* hear God. *Hearing His voice is your gift!*

If you are not sure you are born again you can ask Him right now to take your sins and fill you with His love, forgiveness, and Holy Spirit! He will then lift you to that supernatural place where you have a God consciousness unlike anything in the natural realm.

It is certainly true that some people have a greater inclination to be meditative, to find solace in quiet, and to be sensitive to God's whispers. Obviously, some Christians find it much easier to hear God than other Christians do. However, the key for those who find it more difficult is practice, not resignation. The rewards far outweigh the effort.

Even though you might use the excuse of not being gifted in this area, your biggest obstacle may be that you doubt the truth of what Jesus said – that *you will hear God.* Why don't you hand that doubt to Jesus and give Him a chance to prove you wrong!

> *One of the qualities of being child-like before the Lord is being willing to have new experiences! Give Him permission today to open your spirit in new ways to hear His voice.*

OBSTACLE #5:
WOMEN'S WORK

Although this is certainly akin to Obstacle #4, this partic-ular reason is a big obstacle for some men: *Listening to God and all that meditative stuff is a woman's thing. Men aren't as open to that.* Ooooooh, what about Jesus saying, *"My sheep listen to My voice; I know them, and they follow Me."* (John 10:27) He didn't say, "Some of My sheep listen," or "My ewes listen." Give it up, men! That excuse doesn't fly.

There has been a long tradition in many families that the men carried the mundane responsibilities for the family and the women did the spiritual work. This is certainly not biblical, and it robs families of the model God established and Jesus personified. Fathers are to protect their wives, lead their children, obey and serve God. Jesus sacrificed His life for His bride (the church), led believers into resurrection life, and obeyed the will of the Father to the utmost.

How can a man lead or even love completely, when he does not hear the voice of the One who set the grand plan in motion? Although the Bible is the standard for all behavior, there are cer-tain situations that arise in which a person has to have a personal conversation with the Creator to ask specific questions, to receive reassurance, and to be open for correction. Without this kind of conversational relationship with God it is very hard for a Godly man to lead his family without being rigid and dictatorial. That is not God's way at all.

Generally (and there are many exceptions), women are freer in the intuitive gifts than men. It may be that from child-hood they are more encouraged and blessed in these areas and therefore develop and honor them more. Certainly, sensitivity and intuition in men are not rewarded by the world in most cases. The world demands proof and logic.

Just recognizing that a valuable part of the way he is made by God may be under-used and under-evaluated, is often a helpful release for a man to begin to explore his innate listening abilities.

> *Men, what examples of male*
> *leadership did you have as a child?*
> *What examples are being modeled in your church?*
> *Why not decide to learn from the Creator Himself?*
> *Ask Him today what you need to know!*

OBSTACLE #6:
THE DECEPTION DILEMMA

This one goes back to my tenth birthday. *I've tried to hear God and it's too confusing. What if I hear other voices and am deceived? I can't trust any of them.* My immature reasoning caused me to think I would never be smart enough or discerning enough to know what was really from God and what wasn't. Therefore, I just gave up and missed out on many blessings for the next twenty years.

I realize now that there was another component in my ten year old heart that accompanied my fears of being deceived. My parents' natures were to be very suspicious of anyone and everything. Although they never gave me any instructions about God, their suspicious attitudes were prevalent in our home and erected a dark cloud around seeking spiritual truth. When occasionally my parents would discuss going to church (such as at Christmas and Easter) there was always the admonition to one another that we wouldn't make it a practice and we wouldn't volunteer for anything because "if you get too involved, church people will just use you." It's very revealing for me to remember that the first time I thought about seriously encountering Jesus, I had trust issues, fears, and suspicions about His motives. That idea didn't just appear out of the blue. There were already trust issues set into the DNA of my family.

The primary things that eventually made all the difference in my approach to listening to God were (1) deliberately coming into His presence, (2) being around someone with a contagious expectation to hear God, and (3) having someone willing to teach me the language of the King of Kings.

Together, we are going to learn and practice this language God speaks to us. Sure, we'll make mistakes. All beginners do. Sure, we'll question what we hear. Sure, we'll need correction and exhortation. We'll need to learn to discern God's voice from all the other voices. I'm saying it again: it takes practice. Practice is a part of learning anything well.

Give yourself permission to fail at times but be ready to start again, knowing that you are learning by your mistakes. Use the Bible! Get familiar with its concordance. What is in that book is God's end-all plumb bob for a standard to judge whatever you hear. God will never tell you anything that contradicts Holy Scripture. We'll talk more about this later. For now, just remember: *"If your son asks for bread, will you give him a stone? If he asks for fish, will you give him a snake? If you, even if evil, know how to give good gifts to your children, how much more will your Fa-*

ther in heaven give good gifts to those who ask Him!" (Matthew 7:9-11)

> *Ask Him to speak to your heart!*
> *He wants to!*

OBSTACLE #7:
I'M SCARED

Yes, I've had a few people tell me this: *I'm afraid of what God might say to me! I'd rather not know.* I put this attitude in the same category with the people who have lots of physical symptoms of an illness but won't go to a doctor because they are afraid of what will be discovered. (I've really known these people, too!)

God considers the words He speaks to us so important that He equates *"choosing life over death"* with *"loving the Lord your God, listening to His voice, and holding fast to Him."* (Deuteronomy 30:20)

Conversation is such an important part of our relationship with God that He will lovingly train us, exhort us, discipline us, and direct us so that we will not just "exist" but have "abundant life" through an intimate relationship with Him. We will miss one of the greatest joys of life if we disregard this listening aspect of our relationship with God.

Because it is so easy for any of us to veer off-course at any stage of life, His corrective words can save us a lifetime of heartache. If I am afraid to go to a doctor because of what "might be found wrong," any small problem I have will only escalate in severity if left unchecked and uncared for. If my fears of what

God will say to me prevent me from listening to Him, I may be consigning myself to a lifetime of living beneath my potential, or worse, choosing death rather than life. You may be afraid God will ask you to give up something, or to do something you don't want to do, or will scold you, etc. (When I first began listening to Him, I had the irrational fear that if I totally sold out to Him, He would tell me to be a missionary in Africa against my will and force me to leave everything and everyone I love behind). But I know now that giving up on listening to Him because of fear is cowardly. It is almost always connected to a false understanding of God's character.

How do you picture God? *The Old man upstairs? The Ogre in the sky? The Boss?* Do you think of Him as a *stern, abusive father?* If so, no wonder you are reluctant to hear what He has to say to you! Letting Him teach you **who He is** as well as **what He has to say** may save your life. It's that important!

> *Very honestly, what images do you have of God?*
> *How do these images reflect your intimacy with Him?*
> *What do you fear He may say to you?*
> *Hand Him your fears and dare to listen to what*
> *He says about them!*

Before we move on, let's clarify four Godly actions mentioned in the previous paragraphs:

correction, exhortation, training, and discipline.

Some of you literally cringed inside when you thought of them. Some of you may have shut down or tuned out: *"I'll skip this part."*

Many of us did not grow up with experiences of **loving** discipline or **holy** correction. Instead, it was harsh, demeaning, critical, and embarrassing – sometimes very painful. I totally understand. My concepts were so warped by my personal experiences that when someone, many years ago, recommended to me the fine book by Richard Foster entitled *The Celebration of Discipline*, I shuddered. There was no way I wanted to read such a book. I could not conceive of celebrating any kind of discipline I had ever known.

It took me a while, but when I intentionally began to decide to discover who God really is and put aside my projections of Him from my broken past, He revealed Himself to me in exciting ways. When I determined to hear God's voice instead of the old voices in my life that had wounded me, I found new loving meanings to correction, exhortation, training and discipline. Yes, it took time, but it was so worth the effort! When I finally allowed God to do in me the very things I feared - to correct me, to exhort me, to discipline me, to tell me what to do - I found it to be not fearful at all, but exciting and affirming. I realized that where He took me, when I gave Him permission, was somewhere I had always wanted to go, but had been afraid. (And yes, He even sent me to Africa several times, not as a missionary but as a minister, and He has given me many wonderful African brothers and sisters!)

Choosing to hear God louder than the voices of my past re-defined many words I hated all my life. And the positive experiences I began to have with God affected all my other relationships as well. We'll revisit this subject later in Chapter 21, but if you relate to this fear and reluctance, I just want to encourage you to press in to see what God has in store for you

OBSTACLE #8:
PAST THE EXPIRATION DATE

There is a false teaching that is usually contained within certain denominational walls, however many people who grew up with it continue to let it influence them in irrational ways and rob them of countless blessings. The heresy is that *God doesn't speak to His people anymore. That ended with the apostles.* If you are going to hold onto this tenet, then you have to discount many other scriptures.

For instance: *"Jesus Christ is the same yesterday and to-day and forever."* (Hebrews 13:8) And the prophet's word from God: *"Call to Me and I will answer you and tell you great and unsearchable things you do not know."* (Jeremiah 33:3) Or: *"Therefore, as the Holy Spirit says, 'Oh, that today you would listen as He speaks!'"* (Hebrews 3:7 NetBible)

The reasoning behind not believing that God continues to speak to His people (or continues to perform miracles today) can get sensitive and complicated. Doctrinal teachings go deep into us - especially if we learned them as children and/or from people we loved or looked up to as role models. I strongly suggest that you put this obstacle on the back burner for the moment with respect for those who taught you in the past, while at the same time asking God for yourself whether or not He wants to speak to you. Let Him prove Himself to you. But **you** make the decision to be listening!

These are eight of the most prevalent obstacles people in many different cultures and nations identify when we encourage them to listen to God.

Are there other obstacles / excuses / arguments in your life?
Bring them to the light!

Try This!

I want to invite you to try on an attitude. It may seem very new and different to you. And I hope it seems refreshing! It's more like the attitude of a child I mentioned earlier. Picture this: You are a young toddler, immersed in all the toys and activities you are familiar with, going from one to another throughout your day. Then you are given something new, appealing in a totally unfamiliar, yet irresistible way. You drop all your other interests and concentrate wholeheartedly on this new discovery. You choose to give it your full attention. You are lost in the present moment of unwrapping it, playing with it, turning it over and over, making noises with it, moving it around, pushing all its buttons, speaking into it, putting it up to your ear, tasting it – immersed in its presence!

What if you were to approach intentionally
listening to God just like that!

Of course it's unrealistic that you can put aside **everything** in your life that needs to be done so you can spend time listening to God. We all have responsibilities and many of them are God-given. I already asked you to list those that you feel, as a

Christian, you **should** be doing every day.

> *What are you **actually** doing every day?*
> *What are you feeling a low-grade guilt*
> *about **not** doing every day?*

So, what if ... here's the big question ... what if a lot of the "holy" things you are doing each day (or "holy" things you feel guilty about not doing) are not God's priority for you right now, but are some things you have assumed a follower of Jesus Christ should be doing? What if, for a designated season, you put aside that stack of books someone told you were "must-reads?" What if, for say one month, you don't read your daily devotional every morning, or go through your intercessory prayer list, or some other things you have been doing because you feel God expects you to? What if you temporarily put them aside?

Now, before you start thinking, "Blasphemy!" just try to imagine what God may be offering you instead. What about the opportunity to come into a much more personal, intimate relationship with Him through the art of holy conversation!

Is this worth a try for you? Would you be willing to be that little child for one month in the presence of God? It could be like taking a personal retreat with God without going to a retreat center. Doesn't it sound fun? It could be an irresistible opportunity that will turn into a natural rhythm of your life – once you discover the joy and delight and expectation of hearing His voice regularly. Then everything else you begin to do with Him again (your Bible study, your daily devotions, intercession, etc.) will be enhanced beyond belief.

Find a picture of a toddler that is appealing to you.
Can you identify with this child?
What is it about this child that is admirable?
Keep the picture in a prominent place as a daily reminder to
approach God just like that child approaches life.

CHAPTER 4

PRIORITIES AND PRACTICE

You can't deny the fact that you won't enjoy practicing something that isn't important to you.

My mother thought it was important that I learn to play the piano. So for eight years of my young life I walked to St. Scholastica Convent once a week to take lessons from Sister Celine. I had little interest in playing the piano, and Sister Celine had little interest in teaching me. Her method of instruction was to rap my knuckles with a long stick at every wrong note. Needless to say, I hated practicing, did not do well, and declared for years that I had no talent for the piano. I really never had any motivation to like it, to have fun, to relax with it, and to appreciate the joy of it. It was always a fearful drudgery.

If we are not motivated for an activity, not only will we not have fun with the practice (because practice does get tedious), but we won't be consistent, we'll put it off, and we'll give up easily. This is true in any area you choose: sports, music, cooking, gardening, school, - even spending time listening to God. We enthusiastically practice those things that are important to us and even actually enjoy the tedium because we are doing something thing we love and want to accomplish a measure of expertise. If you love sports, you don't mind the drills; if you love music, you practice the scales; if you love cooking, you master the techniques; if you love gardening, you enjoy the satisfaction of pulling weeds; if you love a subject at school, you even do things for extra credit. If you love being in the intimate presence of God, you spend time listening to what He says and receiving His love.

You don't have to start off in any of these areas with a natural inclination or talent. You may develop an interest in something totally new at any time in your life. This is part of that child-like capacity to embrace wholeheartedly a new source of wonder and delight.

For Instance......

When I was about to reach forty, Conlee asked me what I would like to have for my birthday present on this milestone occasion. To his amazement, I immediately said, "A tennis racquet!" He never expected such a response because he knew how disinterested in sports I had always been. In fact when I was in high school, I always got a doctor's excuse from a family friend to get out of gym class because I didn't want to get hot and perspire. But, after lots of "Are you sure?" questions from Conlee, I turned forty and received a top-of-the-line oversized Prince racquet and lessons from the tennis pro at the neighborhood racquet club.

This was so totally out of my element – but I was motivated! My motive was that I had teen-aged sons who were very athletic by nature. They excelled at every sport they pursued. Because turning forty seemed pretty old to me at the time, I wanted to do something to prove that I was not over-the-hill. I wanted to beat my sons on the tennis court! Looking back, I'm not sure why I chose tennis. Maybe it was because my boys were not tennis players. But it soon became my #1 priority, and I stopped doing lots of other things to have time for it.

I quickly realized that I had no natural affinity for tennis at all. I was so uncoordinated that the pro had me spend the first few lessons just bouncing the ball on my racquet, eventually advancing to hitting it repeatedly against a wall. I had to learn the basics of how to grip the handle properly, how to relax my knees, how to turn my body, how to keep my focus. It wasn't easy for me. But I was motivated! I had a mission: I was going to beat my teen-aged sons!

So I persevered. I practiced every day, timidly joined some leagues of other beginners, gradually advanced to groups of more experienced players, kept going back to my coach, mentally rehearsing serves, back-hands, lobs and volleys when I wasn't on the court. I thought about tennis all the time. I loved it!

It paid off! What I lacked in raw talent, I made up for in technique, finesse, focus and experience. The day came when I challenged my 6'1" and 6'5" sons to a game. They actually laughed when I begged them not to be easy on me. They had never had tennis lessons but assumed that with their natural physical abilities they could easily ace their aging mom. But there I was, returning whatever they served and watching their unbridled brute force hit ball after ball out of the court. I actually beat them quite easily. It was A Moment!

God, Are You My Priority?

Let me tell you a bit about how listening to God and hearing His voice became a priority to me. It is not unlike my choosing to excel in tennis. Perhaps you will make a connection to something that is a priority in your life.

My motivation for wanting to hear God came as soon as I was born again. I was one of those people who didn't just ease into the Kingdom; I arrived with a crash. It was like a parachute drop.

I was thirty-two years old, pretty much settled into a life-style I wanted and loved, happily married to my college sweet-heart, and mother of two healthy sons. We had built our first home in a lovely neighborhood, Conlee owned a growing business, we were active in a prominent church, we belonged to the country club, had a full social life and I was involved in several volunteer service projects. I thought at the time that "this is the best of the best and this is all there is." God was somebody I believed existed, visited on Sunday mornings at church, and didn't think about the rest of the week.

I recently read the following quote from Reinhard Bonnke, the great German evangelist: "Is Christianity boring? So is the best TV program if your set is not plugged in. Be plugged in with God and you won't be yawning!" That perfectly describes where I was – going to church because it was the thing to do but bored with it and bored with what I knew of Christianity. Conlee and I had always been actively involved in any church we attended. For us, that meant we were in lay leadership, but the churches we were involved in seemed more like social clubs. We were also in leadership in the Rotary Club and the Junior League. We were surrounded by people like us, who belonged to church but didn't take it too seriously. I was not "plugged in" to the Source.

However, when out of the blue, I had my personal encounter with the presence of God, I knew **immediately** that He was more real than anything else in my life. There was no comparison. That first taste of His presence was so intense and so incredibly fulfilling that it was impossible for me not to want to know Him as intimately as possible. Just being with Him caused me to come alive in a way I had never experienced.

Initially, one of my biggest fears was that this new awareness of Him would wane, or even vanish over time. After all, I had lived all my life without knowing Him in the biblical way of knowing – that intimate oneness that produces fruit. I wondered if this experience was just a "flash in the pan." A friend in our church even said to me when I shared with her about this new intense awareness of the Lord, "It won't last. I've seen this before and it's a temporary insanity."

When I shared with my parents (who lived in another town) about being born again they were so concerned about me that they contacted two main-line denomination pastors in my hometown and were told by both that this kind of passion for God could lead to insanity and could harm their grandchildren. They recommended psychiatric care.

Friends and family were trying their best to persuade me to back off and return to my old life-style. But my awareness of the presence of God was more real than anything the world had ever offered. Intuitively, I knew that God alone was going to bring healing to the wounds in my heart that went back to childhood. I had been exposed to all that the world offered to compensate for a lack of deep wholeness in my soul and I knew it didn't work. It could distract and it could temporarily comfort, but it had no staying power. In spite of the reactions of those around me, I made a decision to put my life in the hands of the One who heals from the inside out. I was motivated because I wanted to be whole.

Conlee and I were extremely blessed from the beginning of our Christian journey to have a very wise person to mentor and guide us, Leanne Payne.[13]   Leanne first demonstrated the presence of Jesus to us by the way she lived, spoke, acted, and even by her demeanor. Already intrigued with what we saw in her life, we then experienced a revelation of the awesome presence of God for ourselves. He revealed Himself to us in a very dramatic way through roaring sound and blazing fire, much like the account of Holy Spirit coming at Pentecost in Acts 2.[14]

We chose with all our hearts to know Him and follow Him from that time on. Leanne was there to disciple us and to encourage us to move ever deeper into this new walk. Daily, she would ask me the following question: "What did the Lord say to you today?" At first I thought this was the strangest question ever. I would have expected her to ask, "What have you read in your Bible today?" Or, "What did you do for the Lord today?" The idea of expecting Him to speak to me was totally new but intriguing.

Each time she asked, she was very sincere and expected me to have an answer. For days my answer was simply and honestly, "I have no idea." But Leanne modeled for me a Christian who was

13   Leanne Payne founded and led *Pastoral Care Ministries* for many years. She is the author of many fine books which have helped countless people around the world find healing for the soul. She is currently retired. When we first met her in 1972, she was a single mother with a married child on the mission field. Leanne was working on her master's degree in English literature at the University of Arkansas.
14   This event is described in greater detail in *The Journey to Wholeness in Christ*, by Signa Bodishbaugh, Baker/Journey Press, 2008, pages 34-38.

consistently aware of God's presence, intentionally spending time with Him, and listening to what He was whispering in her heart. I saw the fruit of that in her life. I wanted it in mine.

I have to confess that initially my primary motivation for hearing God was the belief that it would keep me on the spiritual "high" that accompanied my introduction to Him. However, that was an immature focus on outward manifestations. As soon as I began to practice listening to God in earnest, I found a depth to my relationship with Him that far surpassed the fireworks of our first encounter. Instead of developing an addiction to the spectacular, I was becoming passionate about knowing God more intimately. I am convinced this is what He wants for each of us.

If I had continued to equate being in God's presence with an intense awareness of the spiritual realm, I would have been tossed back and forth in my spiritual walk like a yo-yo. I can only compare this to the exciting, stimulating, physical reactions a newly married couple has for one another. When, after time, those feelings begin to decrease in their electric intensity and develop into deeper and more meaningful expressions of their love, the marriage matures and the couple actually learns to know one another even more intimately than at first. This doesn't mean that the initial fireworks aren't there often (even after fifty years!) but it means they aren't the focus and they don't determine how much one loves or is loved.

Watching Leanne, who had walked with God for many years, enjoy an intimate, personal way of relating to Him that I didn't have, I immediately saw what I was lacking. She consistently spent quality time with Him, listening and responding. I, too, wanted to be able to communicate with Him in many ways as easily as with my best friend. I, too, wanted to be able to receive

His affirming and loving words that would give a wholesome structure to my life. I, too, wanted to develop a God-consciousness that overcame my self-consciousness. I was so hungry for more of Him that I began to declare in my life, *"I want that!"*

How Much Do I Want That? Let Me Declare My Intentions

I declared my intentions by putting aside a lot of activities I once thought vital. Among them were casual daily phone conversations with friends, recreational shopping, watching TV, reading novels, etc. Ok, you may think these were pretty shallow activities to begin with. But, honestly think about some of the things you do daily without questioning why. It could be reading the morning paper, watching the news, jogging, checking email, looking at Face Book, having coffee with friends, playing a game on your cell phone, etc. They are the things that have become routine for you and perhaps not one of them is bad. They just feed The Huge Looming Obstacle (Time).

What does your daily routine look like?
What do you do most days before noon (when not at work)?
What do you typically do after supper?
How many of these routine activities could instead be opportunities to listen to God?

Periodically, I have to ask God to show me once again where I have started to spend superfluous time that is bearing little fruit. Oh, how easily I can fall into this trap and how quickly The Huge Looming Obstacle chomps away on my life if I'm not careful!

To my amazement, when I focus on God, I don't even miss the things I give up. They pale in comparison. But anytime I fall away from intentionally entering into His presence there appear dozens of tempting ways to fill that time slot.

I declared my intentions by asking for help to hear God's voice. I needed to learn the basics. Hearing Him was not natural to me (as unnatural as holding a tennis racquet was) and at first it seemed only remotely possible. But my goal was to come closer to the God who loved me more than I was ever loved before. I needed His love in my life and I didn't want to miss any opportunity to receive it. I observed others who faithfully spent time in His presence, being shaped by what He spoke to them, and I was hungry for that. I asked for help from Leanne and she gave me some very practical instructions which I will share with you later.

However, the most important thing she told me was to pray – to ask Him to help me hear His voice. So, in a very childlike way, not sure how to pray effectively, I just simply said, *Lord, I love You. I want to know You. Would You speak to me in a way I can understand?*

Although through His Spirit God has equipped me to hear His voice in "fearful and wonderful" ways,[15] I am still woefully inadequate in my own strength. I have learned that it is a sign of great wisdom when we are able to admit, "I can't do this by myself. I need help!" That very admission opens us up wide to the gift

---

15   Psalm 139:14

God sent to us – His Holy Spirit. When we ask, God sends more of the intimate, indwelling presence of His Spirit who enables us in ways we never expect. He helps us to hear God's voice, know God's will, and be empowered to do more than we ever could on our own. He does for us what we cannot do for ourselves.

Help from on high is ours for the asking. It's amazing how quickly we can forget that! When I sit down to listen to God, I just begin to pray, *Lord, I need You! Would You fill me more with Holy Spirit presence today? Would You let Holy Spirit power flow through me as I listen to You?*

It's amazing the difference that makes – every time! When I don't do this it is always a struggle.

I declared my intentions by inviting others to listen with me. I didn't know exactly what a prayer partner was or how to find one or what we would do together. But Leanne said it would be helpful to have "listening prayer partners." So I just began to share my heart with people I already knew. Not all my friends were as excited about my new love for Jesus as I was. In fact, not too many of them were. My parents weren't. Even my pastor wasn't. But my husband was! Conlee became my first prayer partner. Only one of our close couple friends embraced our new love, but they told someone, who told someone, who told someone - and very soon many people we hadn't known previously were coming regularly to our home to share a love of God and a desire to know Him more intimately. It didn't take long before we had more than a listening prayer partner; we had a listening prayer group! It wasn't orchestrated at all. God did it because I asked!

I declared my intentions by purposefully making time each day for Him. I'm not talking about time for doing what I once thought was routine God stuff. I'm talking about intentional time in an intentional place with the intentional purpose to please Him. For instance, I designated a "God Chair" next to a little table where I kept my Bible, Listening Prayer Journal (more about that later), pens, and a place for a cup of coffee. It was also in a location where I enjoyed the view but had the fewest worldly distractions. The time I chose had to be consistent with my family's activities and life-style. Babies in the home, early risers, special activities, etc., all require flexibility with time. Nothing is worse than feeling pressured to have quality quiet time with God in a tight constraint.

Once I settled in my God Chair the format I chose was easy. *God, what do you want to do with me today?* I let Him set the agenda. He always has one!

These were the beginnings of how I set a priority to hear God, and I want to go into each of them in more detail with you. But my how-to list will make little difference in your life unless you establish your own priorities. **Do you really want to hear God for yourself?** Not for the sake of hearing Him speak and receiving some personal revelation, but for coming closer to Him in a relationship that surpasses anything you have ever known?

Listening to God: What are your intentions?
Write out your own priority.

Are you willing to give Him a month?

Make this an agreement with God. Set the dates.
Put it on your calendar, your daytimer, your phone,
or anywhere else where you will be reminded
daily of your intentions.
Look forward to this month as a time of child-like discovery
and adventure with the Creator of the Universe!

What did the Lord say to YOU today?

I will be asking you the same question I was asked as I began.
Expect to hear!
Write it out. You may hear only one word.
You may receive a fleeting impression. Don't ignore it.
You may be tempted to analyze what you hear and
give it your own interpretation. Resist doing this.
Just record what you receive, understanding that
50% of what you hear may be from God and
50% may be from other sources.
This is the way we begin. God is teaching you!

CHAPTER 5

LISTENING 101

When I asked Leanne how I could learn to hear God she not only prayed for me and suggested I ask God also, but she gave me some very practical exercises that I needed to get started. It makes me laugh to think back on some of the things we did individually and as a group when we began because they are much like activities one would use to teach children in a nursery school. However, we professional, well-educated adults were all babes in this endeavor, novices in the Kingdom, and we needed to start simply and bask in the joy of each little accomplishment instead of being pushed into the deep end before we learned how to swim in the Spirit. I will say in all honesty that although what I am going to share with you sounds so elemental and even rather tedious and sometimes downright silly, it was the most fun in the world. These exercises deepened our faith and bore fruit. And these are the very things that have been helpful to so many others as I have shared them with beginning God-listeners over the years. If we had attempted to be sophisticated and imitate the learning techniques of the world, we would have missed the joy of discovering

God's healing love in our lives.

If you make anything too complicated or difficult at the beginning, you will lose most of your students. That is God's wisdom! This is why I spent many beginning tennis lessons just bouncing the ball off my racquet. I did it until I felt comfortable and the racquet began to feel natural in my hand. This is the same principle God used with the Israelites off on their Great Adventure to the Promised Land after the Exodus. He gave them many instructions through Moses. Everything was new and unnatural to each one of them who had been slaves in Egypt all their lives. All they knew was menial labor, assembly-line-like tasks of gathering straw and mud, making bricks, hauling materials, setting bricks in place, etc. They did the same things day after day, and it had been that way for 400 years.

When God led them out of their rat race, they must have been overwhelmed. Every day He led them into experiences they probably never thought of before. They went places they had never been, were asked to do things they had never done, met challenges they had never encountered. But God capped off all of His instructions to them with this comforting word. *"What I am commanding you today is not too difficult for you or beyond your reach .... The word is very near you; it is in your mouth and in your heart so you may obey it."* (Deuteronomy 30:11, 14)

Life without God at the center is much like the assembly line living of the Israelites in Egypt. You do what is expected by those who influence you or have control over you. But once you give the Lord control of your life you are living on the edge, not really knowing or expecting what will come next. He always has surprises and challenges and revelations. This is an exciting life, but it can be overwhelming as well. He asks us to do things we have never done before, perhaps never thought of before. He wants us to grow into the people He created us to be. In every instance, His ancient, eternal word applies to us today: *This is not too difficult for you or beyond your reach. I am the Living Word and I am in you!*

K.I.S.S. (Keep It Simple Stupid) was a popular motto in the U.S. Army when Conlee served early in our marriage. However, there is always the fine line between keeping something simple enough for everyone to learn it, yet not being so boring that many will lose interest, tune out, and quit. God proves to us that He can keep the basics of hearing His voice very simple, yet make it the most exciting adventure we've ever had. That is a Divine Plan!

Back to Basics

One night as our new little group of believers met at our house to be in God's presence together, Leanne asked us all to sit on the floor in a circle. She assigned a short scripture to us. Because we all had new Bibles and were just learning how to negotiate them, it took some time for everyone to find the right place. She was very patient. There were several versions and translations of the Bible among us and each one was read aloud. We all commented on the various nuances but agreed that the meaning was the same in each. Then she asked God to speak to our hearts about the Word we just read. She told us that we should seek a personal application from the scripture that God would apply to us individually. She encouraged us to relax, not to strive to get something profound, but just to be aware that God was in our midst and to be in tune with whatever He gave. Then, for whatever He imparted to our hearts or imaginations, to be thankful. Although I was unaware that I had ever heard God speak to me before, this sounded easy and interesting. No pressure. No unrealistic expectations.

Until..., then she said that after a few moments of listening we would go around the circle and each one of us would share what we heard God say. I nearly died! I just knew I would be the only one who heard nothing. Maybe she'd let me pass. But oh, no! As soon as that thought entered my mind, Leanne said there would be no passes because God was speaking to each of us and each of us would hear something from Him. We just needed practice to recognize His voice.

So, our circle of listeners got very quiet. Suddenly a little more nervous, we looked back over the scripture we had just read aloud. I tried to focus on hearing God say the scripture to me, trying to imagine what He sounded like, really wanting to know how He would apply it to my life. But - nothing. The time we spent in quiet seemed to go on and on and on. I began to hear a children's song playing in my head and I couldn't get rid of it. Have you ever had a tune go through your mind so long you thought you'd go crazy? This was like that. I was so put out with myself because it was preventing me from hearing what God wanted to say. But, over and over and over, it played inside me. *Jesus loves me, this I know. For the Bible tells me so.....*

All the while, here's what was going on in my thoughts: *I'm so stupid. My parents always told me I was stupid. Why did I ever think I could do this? I'll fail at this. I'll be the only one here who won't hear God. I've reverted back to childhood and that silly little Sunday School song. I can't get it out of my head.*

I can't believe I ever thought God would speak to me. What if Leanne makes me go first? I'll be mortified. No matter how hard I tried to focus on the scripture and on God, my thoughts were all over the place. And still, the tune persisted.

Finally, Leanne said it was time for us to share what God said to us. To my great relief she asked a man across from me to go first. Like so many of us often do, he began with apologies. "Well, this is probably just me. I'm not sure this was God, but I just seemed to be aware that God was saying ..... He loves me."

Excitedly, the woman next to him began to exclaim, "You know, I'm pretty sure I heard God say He loves me. It was such a simple thing I almost missed it, but the impression of knowing it just sort of filled me up somehow."

Then two or three other people shared the same thing: "Jesus loves me." It was unanimous.

"Signa," Leanne finally said, "you haven't said anything. What did God say to you?" All I could do was sing aloud, *Jesus loves me this I know. For the Bible tells me so...*

This simple song brought a profound and totally unexpected revelation to me that night when I listened to God. In the one little phrase that resonated through my thoughts came a truth, along with a confirmation from the others in the room, that Jesus indeed loved me when I was a child. He loved me when I didn't know Him; He loved me when I was afraid; He loved me when I felt alone. He loved me through people He had put in my life. And now He was confirming it in His written Word and through a personal word in my heart. I was absolutely filled up with His presence and a new awareness of His love.

Reflecting on this initial listening experience I learned several principles that apply all the time:

- God speaks to me in many ways, not always like I expect.
- A single word or phrase from Him can carry a life-time of meaning and healing.
- The Bible is God's definitive Word for all believers.
- His indwelling presence dispels all fears of being deceived.
- God's words to me overcome my inadequacies.
- One simple experience with God fills me with a plumb-less depth of love.
- Listening prayer partners help confirm God's word to me.
- I **can** hear God!

CHAPTER 6

THE ULTIMATE, END-ALL, FINAL, DECISIVE, DEFINITIVE, VITAL, REFERENCE BOOK

On the day I was born again I don't think I had ever read more than a few isolated scriptures or basic stories in the Bible outside of being in church. What's more shocking is that we must have acquired at least a dozen Bibles that rested on assorted shelves in our home. I had several with my name embossed on the front cover, gifts from people for rites-of-passage occasions. I still had the one my grandmother gave me on my tenth birthday. One had belonged to my great-great-grandfather, Elder McBride from Ireland. And one was a large family Bible with important dates penned in the front. They had sentimental value to me but no spiritual value. I couldn't have told you the relationships between Abraham, Isaac and Jacob or who the prophets were or who wrote letters in the New Testament. I just wasn't interested.

But then God........! Belonging to Him, falling in love with

Him, identifying with Him, and becoming a citizen of His Kingdom changed everything! Almost overnight I acquired a passion
for learning the Word of God. Again, I had to assume the posture
of a little child, not a college student. So instead of enrolling in a
graduate study of the Bible at the local university, I went to kin-
dergarten.

There was so much I didn't know that I had no idea how
to start. Oh, over the years I occasionally had the notion that it
would be good to read through the Bible on my own because it
was an important work of literature that had survived thousands
of years. I had studied Chaucer and Old English literature; I had
majored in French and spent months reading Medieval French
literature. I knew The Bible had scholastic merit, too, so I attempted to read it from time to time. Of course I always started
with Genesis 1 in a King James Version and maybe got through
the Adam and Eve story – or maybe not. It seemed disjointed to
me, and although I have always been a voracious reader, it just
did not hold my interest.

Occasionally I had taken courses offered in our church on
how to study and read The Bible. These, too, did not hold my interest. They were led either by our pastor or university professors
who attended our church. There were basically three ways these
Bible studies were led. Very briefly, this is how we were taught to
read The Bible: (1) Through the lens of higher criticism we were
taught to analyze and dissect verses in order to decide with our
human wisdom what was inserted later, what was true, and what
was superstition. I came to the same conclusion I did as a ten year
old. *I am not smart enough to do this.* (2) Through the lens of
documentary hypothesis we were taught about the Yahwist inclusions (J), the Elohist inclusions (E), the Deuteronomist entries

(D), and the Priestly references (P). The Bible became like a big puzzle that had to be sorted out in intricate ways before you could ever understand it. *This is way too complicated.* (3) Through the lens of form criticism we were taught to interpret scripture according to its literary content: Is it prose, poetry, history, etc, and as such, how should it be interpreted or valued? *Who am I to make such judgments of value?*

In none of these studies were we ever invited to see the scriptures as the Word **of** God. We were studying the Bible as words that man had written **about** God and deciding for ourselves if they were relevant and/or true. For many reasons these were dangerous ways to approach the Bible. Perhaps the most dangerous of all was that it cut the heart out of the Word and it cut the heart out of those of us who studied.

But now that I was born again, there was a fire burning in **the new heart** God gave me. I was motivated in an entirely different way to know God's Word. I wanted to know what He was saying to me! I wanted to apply the Bible to my own life! This was so exciting because I now knew the Author!

I searched out some of the newer translations of the Bible and even some of the paraphrases that made it easier to understand and more personal. I was fascinated to learn that some of the newer versions were more accurately translated than the much revered King James Version due to later discoveries of ancient Biblical manuscripts. I sensed that God really wanted to give every opportunity for people to understand the eternal messages coming through His Word.

I was told that there was a Christian bookstore on the square in our town and that the owners would be helpful to a new believer. I had never seen the bookstore. All the times I shopped in stores around the square, I just passed it by. But, there it was, nestled between the department store and the bank – The Church Mouse! So one day I went in, feeling very out of place, and timidly told the lady at the counter that I was brand new at all this but wanted to learn The Bible as a believer.

I was surprised at how delighted she was for me, not just to sell me a Bible, but she seemed genuinely excited that I was recently born again. How different her reaction was from most of my close friends, or even my parents and my pastor! About an hour later I left the shop with *The Jerusalem Bible, Good News for Modern Man, The Living Bible,* and two sets of Bible study booklets, one for me and one for Conlee. Plus, I felt I had a new friend in the store owner, who had just prayed for me on the spot, and given me the promise of a mature Christian support group who would embrace and encourage me.

The study course I brought home that day was a set of ten little booklets called *Studies in Christian Living*, with a basic fill-in-the-blanks format, published by The Navigators. I still have these booklets that I pored over that first month, devouring all the information I could about the Word of God. Their 1972 price is still on them; they were 45 cents apiece! For me, they were priceless!

The little booklets were extremely simple and oriented from the position that God inspired every word in the whole Book and that He would apply all of it to my life if I asked Him to. This study got me moving through the whole Bible, becoming familiar with the different books, looking up scriptures to answer the questions, seeing the totality of the Word, and learning the character of God. I discovered that the Bible is about one God from Genesis to Revelation (not an Old Testament God and a New Testament God), revealed through one Son in the Person of Jesus, and one Spirit, and is full of many promises for me. As Conlee and I went through these studies we were encouraged to:

- Read the Bible every day with a regular plan
- Pray every day
- Attend a believing church regularly
- Tell others about Jesus

These four recommendations became a part of our lives without striving. The most difficult point for us (and the one that took us the longest to achieve) was about the importance of attending a believing church. From the beginning of our spiritual awakening we openly shared what God was doing in our lives with our pastor and friends in our church. We were ridiculed and ostracized by some. We were told that we were not being true to our tradition by others.

We volunteered to teach the high school Sunday School class, a class no one ever wanted to tackle. Almost to a person, each one who attended was there because a parent insisted, bribed, or threatened. These young people were not interested in being in church, and were definitely not interested in studying the Bible. We bought each student a copy of *Good News for Modern Man* and began with a study of the book of Mark. It was short, concise, and we felt it was a good place for them to begin. The only time we had their attention was the day we told them our testimony, about how God appeared to us in a supernatural way. We felt a glimmer of hope for the kids, but it was thwarted. As soon as some of their parents found out what we were doing they asked the pastor to "fire" us from the position. They said we were talking too much about Jesus and they would "rather their kids do drugs than become Jesus freaks."

Rumors and gossip about what Conlee and I were doing took on a life of their own. We were accused of being in a cult, of holding séances, and of losing our minds. Although influenced with the popular idea of the day to "bloom where you are planted," we finally realized that the soil of this church was polluting our lives and our children. We had to do something.

We did not act rashly, but waited until God made it perfectly clear that He was releasing us from the church we had invested in for many years. We began to attend a small neighborhood church, first on Monday nights for "Prayer and Praise" services and on Sunday mornings, until He said to make the move. By this time, we thought the people in our old church would be glad to get rid of us, but our move was not well-received. Our pastor said he felt we had betrayed him. Many of the people no longer invited us to their social gatherings and hardly spoke in public. Yet, God provided us with a place growing by leaps and bounds with like-minded, displaced main-line church members, who were yielding to the power of Holy Spirit during the Charismatic Renewal of the '70's. It was so exciting! We saw and participated in miracles, transformations, deepening faith, and were given opportunities to minister within the church and beyond.

Although those first Navigator booklets we studied did not mention specifically listening to God's voice, they did introduce me to the living Word of God. By becoming grounded in His Word, I was establishing The Plumb Line I always need for hearing Him. I had to ask Conlee, my engineer husband, to demonstrate a plumb bob for me. I've heard the term "plumb" forever, but wasn't really sure what it meant. He took a pointed weight, attached a string to it, and hung it from a hook. After a few seconds it quit swaying and became absolutely vertical, true every time. Accurate measurements can be taken from such a precise line, without questioning its correctness. There is no need to question it because it establishes the standard.

This is what the Word of God, The Bible, is for all God-listeners. Every time we listen to God speak to us in a personal voice, we measure what we hear by our Divine Plumb Line. God is consistent and we can put all our trust on whatever lines up with His Word. Like a plumb bob, it is absolutely true every time. We can accurately measure truth by His standard without questioning or using any other standard of measurement. What a relief! This gives me permission to listen to Him in confidence and in peace, without trying to analyze everything in depth with questions like: *Is this me or is it God? Is it something I just heard somewhere or is it really God's truth to me?*

How different this approach is from the one I was taught in our former church! Instead of approaching The Word from a standard of analysis and doubt, like a science project, I began with a completely different attitude. I would not wait until God proved to me that His Word was true to accept it; I would **begin with the assumption of its veracity and see what happened.** Not only did this go against Conlee's training as an engineer and my natural instincts to doubt, but it went against all the religious instruction we had received.

However, I looked at the fruit in the lives of those who dissected the Word until they cut the heart out of it. Then I looked at the fruit in the lives of my new acquaintances who accepted God for who He says He is, and put their weight on Him more and more each day. There was no comparison!

Approaching The Bible with an open, accepting attitude (the child-like posture) became much more than a study time. I was infused with a supernatural passion for letting it change me. I realized that this new attitude was not just something I decided to do, but now that Jesus was living inside me, He was motivating me from the inside out. No longer did I approach The Bible like it was an insect on a dissecting board, but like a treasure chest of great wealth to be opened and enjoyed.

Within a couple of weeks after my initial encounter with the Lord, I was not only committed to listen to God's voice, I was committed to study The Bible! What incredible changes were taking place in my life! It didn't take long for us to find organized, believing Bible studies around town. How exciting to be with people who were hungry like we were for more of God through studying His Word!

> *What Bible studies have you really enjoyed?*
> *What made them profitable for you?*
> *Are you currently involved in a good study?*
> *If not, ask God to help you find one!*

CHAPTER 7

A LISTENING PRAYER JOURNAL

I have been keeping Listening Prayer Journals[16] for over forty years. I know exactly where they are and I can put my finger on any day's entry if you give me a little time. For a person who can't find her reading glasses most of the time, this is quite remarkable. The main reason why this is has always been such an important part of my life is because when I came into the Kingdom I thought it was a requirement. Following on the heels of Leanne's persistent, daily question, "What did God say to you today?" was the exhortation, "Now write everything He says in your Listening Prayer Journal." So, from the beginning of my New Life my little list of must-have prayer equipment was — and still is:

- A Bible
- A pen
- A Journal

---

16   I consistently capitalize *Listening Prayer Journal* with the deliberate intention of separating such a notebook from all other kinds of journals one might keep.

It's really pretty simple (K.I.S.S.). And when you get established, old habits stick with you forever. To this day when I really want to hear God speak, or if I sense He wants to say something to me, I automatically grab my Bible in one hand and my Journal in the other.

Obviously, that's not as easy for everyone. I know some men and women who would almost rather have a root canal than have to intentionally listen to God and write down what He says. If you're one of these, oh, how I hope I can help you find some delight in listening and journaling!

It is evident that journaling has become more and more popular for Christians because you can just look in any Christian bookstore, and you'll find shelves and racks of journals available in all sorts of styles. Some are thematic with scriptures on each page. Some are beautiful, some very masculine, lined or unlined. Some are expensive and some are only spiral notebooks or loose leaf binders. But journaling is not a modern concept; in fact the practice is ancient. Whether written on papyrus, parchment or notebook paper, keeping a journal has been practiced since writing began to replace oral tradition.

In modern times we have greatly altered the Biblical examples of journaling. We have become much more subjective and introspective, spending hours (or pages) on our feelings about things rather than on what God is saying to us. Of course it's important, and even therapeutic, to express our feelings. It's so much healthier than keeping them bottled up and festering inside. However, the object of a Listening Prayer Journal (which is what I want to encourage you to keep) is **dialogue**. Before we get into the specifics of how to begin and continue a Listening Prayer

Journal, I will digress a bit to make sure we are on the same page with one another about dialogue with God.

Dialogue

Dialogue is NOT monologue! Dialogue is a conversation, a chat, a discussion, an exchange of ideas. Dialogue involves response, reaction and replies. It is active. There is energy in dialogue. Two or more enter into dialogue with liveliness and vigor. It is not stagnant, dead-end, or motionless. Dialogue goes somewhere.

Prayer is a part of dialogue with God. God initiates the dialogue and the prayer part is what we say to Him.[17] Although primarily God is the initiator, He also responds to the prayers of His people. **He is the God who hears the cries of His people and does something!** Let's look at the Word of God to see how this happens.

One of my favorite examples of how God hears and responds to His people is found in Exodus 2:23-25. The Israelites have been in slavery in Egypt for four hundred years. They groan and cry out to God for help. They are desperate. Their lives are miserable. God **hears** their cries. This "hearing" is the Hebrew word *shema*. The word implies that not only does one hear, one

---

17   God is always the initiator. Although we often feel that we cry out to God before He chooses to speak to us, in reality He is constantly speaking and inviting us to have a conversation with Him. We tend to set aside time and go to a specific place and begin a dialogue. Then we wait to see if God will respond. But it is God who prompts us to seek His face. He awakens our hearts to desire to know Him. It frequently takes a crisis in one's life to become interested in what He wants to say, but He is waiting for us to come, no matter how long it takes or what the motivation is. See 1 John 4:19.

responds. In fact the same word *shema* means both "to hear" and "to obey" (or respond) at the same time. It is not a "pick-and-choose-according-to-the-context" definition. *Shema* means that when one hears, one does something. One does not ignore what one hears. There is also a depth of meaning here that goes beyond mere audio reception.

Then the account in Exodus says that God **remembers** His covenant (promise) with Abraham, Isaac and Jacob. The Hebrew word for "remember" is *zakhor* which also has a greater implied depth of meaning, much more than just a mental recollection. God doesn't just think about the promises He made to His people, He actually enters into the covenant as if it is being established at that very moment. He is so present to every moment in time that every aspect of it is alive. It is an ongoing action.

Then the Word says that God looks on His people and **knows** them (or some translations say, "is concerned about them"). This is the Hebrew word *yada*. Oh, the meaning in this word is so beautiful and so intense it is a shame we water it down so! *Yada* implies a "knowing" where two come together in love to the extent that they become one. Out of their oneness new life is conceived and fruit comes forth. It is the word used to describe the love union of Adam and Eve in the physical realm in Genesis 4:1. It is the word God uses to describe His relationship with His people. This is the same meaning Jesus gives to New Life and making disciples.[18] It is what happens the moment we enter into

---

18   In Matthew 7:23, Jesus tells those who have prophesied, driven out demons, and performed miracles that they cannot enter the Kingdom of Heaven because, "I never *knew* you." This word in Greek is *ginosko*. It has the same meaning as the Hebrew word *yada*. Jesus is saying to those who would follow Him that there is more to Kingdom living than doing the right things. Receiving New Life and becoming His disciple means that we come to Him in such an intimate way that we become one and bear fruit from our relationship.

a covenant with Him – He "knows" us! We become one with Him and we are able to bear fruit.

All of these descriptions of how God related to the Israelites in Exodus 2 apply to **you!**

- *Shema* - He hears you!
- *Zakhor* - He responds to your prayer!
- *Yada* - He is intimately connected to you through the covenant you made with Him and New Life is conceived in you so that you will bear much fruit!

How exciting is that!

HTZ vs DTZ

Now, before you start coming up with examples of how you prayed for something so fervently and you felt like God did NOT respond, let's talk about God's DIVINE TIME ZONE (DTZ) and our HUMAN TIME ZONE (HTZ).

HUMAN TIME ZONE is natural to us and we are used to its limitations. We may not like the limitations, but they are familiar and HTZ is our constant default position. We assume that there are going to be somewhat familiar limits of time between requests and answers. We are conditioned by human customs and experiences to expect reasonable responses from others. If I call you on the phone, I expect a "hello" from your end within a few seconds of your connecting. If I ask you a question, I expect some kind of a reply almost immediately, even if it is, "I don't know." We consider this to be civil behavior and part of our natural human relationships with one another.

Our HTZ point of reference changes with technology. Can you imagine living in the days of the Pony Express? I would write you a letter that might take three months to reach your hands. Then, if you answered it promptly, it would take another three months for me to receive your response. Today, most of us even get a bit irritated if someone doesn't return an email or a phone call within twenty-four hours.

Our HTZ also involves living in *Chronos (χρόνος)*, the Greek word for numeric or limited (chronological) time. Besides being limited by our own expectations, we are limited by the number of seconds, minutes and hours in a day and days in a year and years in a life. All of this establishes a zone in which we live as humans. It is our HTZ. Each person on earth is equally given twenty-four hours every day. The President of the United States, the Pope, and the beggar on the street corner all experience the same limitations of time. The quality of HTZ is determined by the choices we make.

But the exciting time zone where God dwells (which really isn't time at all) we call *Kairos (ΚΑΙΡΟΣ)*, the Greek word for God's DIVINE TIME ZONE. *Kairos* literally means "the right or opportune moment."

When you open your heart in prayer to God, He responds immediately and manifests His response to you in the perfect, most opportune moment – **from His perspective.** Perhaps it doesn't seem like the perfect timing **from your perspective,** but His DTZ is always on the mark. What we want to receive from Him may not (usually does not) come at the moment we think it should according to HTZ or our own agenda. But the absence of

His immediate response in human time does not mean that He did not hear, does not care, or is not responding.

Rather, from the moment your prayer leaves your heart, He is actively involved in every detail, speaking into each situation, wanting you to experience His love and His concern for you personally. He just sees each detail of your situation much more clearly than you ever can.

What a fresh and freeing way to pray! To imagine my chronological concerns and needs being received by God in His DIVINE TIME and answered at just the right moment from the perspective of The All Wise One!

A stunning example of this came shortly after God called Conlee into full-time ministry. The call was personal, unmistakable, and set our hearts on fire to get on with it. Yet, circumstances, people in authority positions, and seminary requirements kept us waiting for months and months on end. Knowing that we had to sell our home, sell Conlee's business, make a move to a seminary that required three years of training and a Master of Divinity degree to be earned, find a new house, and find a new school for our one son still at home, it all seemed daunting.

One Sunday in a church service I was crying out (complaining) to God: *Lord, we weren't looking for this call, but You put a passion in our hearts for ministry and yet nothing is happening. We are just on hold. You called us, we said yes, and then You backed off. Why aren't You doing something? Why is it taking so long? We have things to do. We're ready now!*

His answer came to me suddenly and humbled me beyond description: *I am preparing a place for you. It is the perfect place where I want you to be. If you get ahead of My plans, it will disrupt all that I know is best for you.*

Not until years later did we realize that in the waiting time before ministry God was choreographing an amazing opportunity. He prepared an assistant pastor in Mobile, Alabama (a place we had never been), to move to another church. This man's move opened a staff position in a church that had just recently become receptive to the ministry of healing and reconciliation that God was calling us to. In the exact month when Conlee was ready to find a church after his graduation and internship from seminary, the assistant pastor moved. Exactly two weeks later a mutual friend introduced Conlee via telephone to the senior pastor of the Mobile church. An instant connection was made, Conlee and I visited Mobile, interviewed, and he was hired. Later, the church leaders said that they had no intentions of hiring anyone to fill the position so soon, but it was obvious that God had opened the door and they recognized it was His will. God had faithfully prepared a place for us, where the ministry He had been preparing us for would be welcomed and fruitful. If we had usurped His DTZ with our HTZ agenda, we would have missed a multitude of blessings and a ministry for over twenty years with this congregation.

I'll share another example that may seem to be a trifling way to illustrate this grand relationship we have with the Creator. However, my point is that The Almighty One is intimately involved in **whatever** concerns His children, no matter how insignificant it may seem to someone else.

We have this dog, Ramsey, a small black Lab. Most of the time, she is the sweetest, gentlest, most well-behaved dog that you will ever see. She sits on command; she doesn't beg for food at the table; she goes to her bed when told; she sleeps all night;

and she sits quietly at the door until you let her outside to the fenced backyard. But there is one major flaw in Ramsey. If she sees open spaces, she runs as fast as she can and will not obey any commands to come, sit or stay. A door or gate left ajar to the wide open spaces becomes the opportunity she lives for. Off she goes! She eventually becomes disoriented, loses all sense of direction, and is hopelessly lost. She has run off many times, missing for up to two weeks, and then someone will find her, call the number on her tag, and bring her home. I call her Ramsey with the Wayward Heart. Needless to say, Ramsey is grounded for life!

Recently she discovered a loose board in the backyard fence and made one of her great escapes. We didn't notice she was gone for several hours. For days we drove up and down the roads, calling, looking, asking, praying. Nothing happened. I was at the point of giving up. It had been over two weeks, the longest she'd ever been missing and I was thinking this was going to be the time she would not be found and returned. I was even planning how I would recover the outdoor furniture she sleeps on when she's on the back porch.

And then, early one morning during my quiet time with the Lord, I heard this from Him in my spirit: *This is the day Ramsey comes home.* I was stunned. I had given up hope. I had prayed so fervently the first few days for her safety and her return. I had even quit praying. I wrote God's words in my Listening Prayer Journal and dated it with the exact time, and shared it with Conlee. All day we looked outside, called her, drove around searching once again. Nothing. At first I had expected to see her at any moment, but it was getting later and later, almost dark with no sign of our wayward dog. Then just before sunset, when I was beginning to wonder if I had heard God correctly, a car drove up to our gate. Out stepped a beautiful young blonde woman covered from neck to toe in colorful tattoos. Just as I was opening the door to ask what she needed, she led Ramsey on a leash from the back seat of her car! I was overjoyed! I was thrilled that Ramsey was home once again, but I was especially excited that God had spoken to me and that He had been intimately involved in the homecoming.

I ran outside and effusively threw my arms around the startled woman in gratitude. In a rush of words and emotion, I told her that God had spoken to me that morning and that He used her to answer my prayers. She looked a little doubtful about that, but told me she had the dog for several days waiting for the vet, whose number was on Ramsey's tag, to call her back. She left as quickly as possible, refusing to take a reward, saying she had to get back to work at the tattoo parlor. I think she may have been afraid of what this crazy God-lady might do next. But maybe, she had found Ramsey because God orchestrated it so that she could know that God used her to answer prayer and accomplish His will! I pray that God will use that experience in her life.

This is such a simple example of trusting God when a response seems delayed, but if we pay attention, we can learn volumes from our simplest experiences. When a response from God is delayed for days, weeks, months, or even years, it is so easy for us to assume He is not listening, doesn't care, or that His silent answer is automatically "no." When we hear a response from Him and it doesn't come to pass when we think it is time, we will question ourselves as I began to do about Ramsey.

Keeping a Listening Prayer Journal is a hugely effective way to dissuade those false accusations. Looking back at my years of written dialogues with God and seeing the intricate ways

He works in the situations of my life over time is incredibly faith building. I am in awe of the unexpected ways He has intervened in my concerns, large and small. Sometimes He responds in an action and sometimes with an encouraging word to me. But I have learned from experience. **He always responds!**

Write It Down!

Biblically, when God asked His people to write down something, it was because He spoke to their hearts and wanted them to give appropriate importance to what they heard Him say. He wanted them to cherish and value the words they heard from Him. I can relate to this because seeing in my own handwriting the visible evidence of what I hear in my heart from God gives the words significance and helps establish them for His purposes. They become more than something I hear today and forget tomorrow.

I have found it very important to write out the impressions, words, thoughts, or pictures He gives me **exactly** as I receive them. If I attempt to edit, analyze, or embellish what I receive, I will lose the essence of His presence in the dialogue. There is certainly an appropriate time when that critical part of listening is important - when I ask Him questions and request clarifications. But what I first receive from Him is important to remember and should be preserved somehow in an undiluted way.

When He speaks to me, it is because, through our shared conversation, He is changing me, little by little, into a better person – the one He created me to be.

Here are some Biblical examples:

When God gave the Israelites commandments that would change their lives He told them to:

> *Impress them on your children,*
> *Talk about them at home,*
> *Wear reminders of them on your person,*
> *Write them on your homes.*
>
> (Deuteronomy 6:6-9)

Whatever it took, God wanted His words to His people to find a resting place in their lives. God speaks words to His people so that they will have abundant life.

> *His words will be as the apple of your eye.*
> *Bind them on your fingers.*
> *Write them on the tablet of your heart.*
>
> (Proverbs 7:1-3)

The Lord says: "*Write down the revelation I give you and make it plain on tablets.*" (Habakkuk 2:2)

What If I Hadn't Been Listening?

In dialogue at least two parties speak equally. It doesn't mean that one person is not the leader or the initiator; dialogue implies that everyone involved has a voice. God wants dialogue with you! He wants you to pour out your heart to Him, holding back nothing. But, as much as you need to have someone who will listen to you with compassion and understanding, He wants you to hear Him. His words to you will bring you life today, just as He promised in ancient days. Don't miss what He has to say!

I vividly remember a man, Blake, who came for prayer many years ago. He was having serious problems in his marriage and was intent on justifying his own actions and proving that his wife was the cause of all their difficulties. He seemed to want Biblical justification for blaming her for all their marriage woes. After listening to him for a few minutes, we began to pray. God's word came to me very quickly for him: *Blake, I want you to start listening to Me instead of your own pain and self-righteousness.* Wow! That was a harsh word, but he seemed to accept that it was a word from God.

We talked at length about designating time for intentional listening to God and keeping a Listening Prayer Journal. He was pretty doubtful that he would be able to do it, but since he was desperate, he said he would give it a try.

A few weeks later I heard from him. Here is what he said in a letter:

> *Dear Signa,*
>
> *I honestly left our prayer session thinking that what you suggested was something for women. I didn't know one man who did that sort of thing. But you seemed so sure that God had give you that word for me and that keeping a listening prayer journal would help that I decided to give it a try for a week. Boy, was I surprised! I didn't expect to hear God. But He started to show me stuff about myself, not about my wife. He showed me where I'd been hurt, even in my childhood, and blamed her. The bottom line is that she and I have started talking and that's a miracle. I can show her things I write down during my listening time. I think there's hope.*
>
> *Thanks for helping me get started with this. All I can say is: What if I hadn't been listening?*
>
> *Blake*

Getting Started

Here's a good way to start if this is new to you:

- ### *Get a Listening Prayer Journal that you will use.*

   If you don't already have one, get one today! Don't get one like someone else got, or even use one that was a gift if it doesn't feel comfortable to you. Get one that is uniquely suited for you. I started out with the pretty ones, but fairly early on I graduated to a simple loose leaf binder. Sometimes I put topic dividers in mine. However, right now I am using a small one I can carry easily because we travel a good bit. The one you will use consistently has to fit your life-style and your personality. It's a good idea to ask God to help you choose. He has an investment in this too!

   If you have been keeping a journal but it is filled with your outpourings of negativity and pain, consider starting a new one that you will intentionally use to hear what God is saying as much as writing out your feelings and needs.

- ### *Get a pen that will write easily.*

   This may sound silly, but it's hard to write without distraction if the pen doesn't feel comfortable in your hand and doesn't flow with your style of penmanship. Keep it attached to your journal. I am aware that in this electronic age some people keep a prayer journal on the computer or on an electronic tablet. I don't like to do this because it feels less personal to me, but that's your choice. However you do it, just do it!

- ### *Each time you begin, ask God to speak to your heart in a way you will recognize.*

Remember my prayer: *Speak to my heart, change my life, and make me whole.* You are expecting God to communicate with you. You believe that whatever He says will make a difference, a change in you. And you believe that whatever change He makes is for your good and will make you whole.

- *To "break in" the first page, write the heading: WHO I AM IN CHRIST*

    You don't have to do this, but it's a great idea for a beginner. Begin by asking God to name you. By this, I mean that He has names for you that define who you are in His eyes. They may be names He gives to all of His children such as *Beloved, Friend, Brother, Sister,* or *Child.* Or He may give you specific names that describe certain qualities He loves in you. Just listen to what He says and write them down without arguing, questioning or disbelieving. The names (qualities, definitions, attributes, identity) that He speaks to your heart about how He sees you are His opinion, perhaps not yours.[19] Honor what He says. Hear in your heart how He perceives you, and then see in your own handwriting what He says about you. Every day as you begin to listen to Him, start here and begin to see your first page fill up with God's perspective of who you are.

- *If you are doing a daily devotional or reading a portion of scripture each day, start here.*

    Then ask God to speak to you about what you just read.

------

19   God sometimes described a person by what he would become, not where he was in the moment. For instance, He called Abraham, "father of many nations," before he had a child. He called Gideon, "mighty warrior," when Gideon was still hiding out in fear in a winepress. He called Simon, "Cephas" or "Peter," which means "rock," even though He knew Peter would deny Him three times.

Hear Him reading it to you. Insert personal pronouns where applicable. *What are You saying to me through this today, Lord?* Read until He causes a word, phrase or idea to resonate within you. Stop right there and ask Him how that applies to you.

- ***Pour out your heart to Him – your love, thanksgivings, concerns, needs, etc.***

     This is a time to remove your filters, to let your raw emotions flow from your heart to His. Write out some of the more significant points that come from you and from Him. You don't have to prepare a well-organized presentation for God. Rather, it's an outpouring of who you are in the depths of your being. Whatever response to what He says that occurs in your mind or emotions, ask Him about it. He may give you a word or impression that leads to another question, then another, and another. He may clarify some things that have been confusing. He may ask you questions you had not considered. He may encourage you or re-direct you. Write out what He gives. This kind of flow produces meaningful dialogue. You find you will gradually begin to listen with your heart rather than with your rational mind.

     Prayer is not intended to be an extended worry session.

- ***Date each entry.***

     This will greatly assist you whenever you want to go back to an important word you received. Often what He speaks to us in the past serves as a confirmation in the future.

     One of the biggest challenges many people have in keeping a Listening Prayer Journal is the temptation to edit and organize their entries before writing from the heart. Editing is for publishing, not for keeping a heart record of your dialogues with God.

This is not for anyone to see but you.

Above all, remember: This is an adventure with God. It's fun! It's not a chore!

> *What did the Lord say to you today?*
> *Be sure to write it in your Listening Prayer Journal!*
> *How is your God Month going?*
> *Are your priorities lining up with His?*
> *How many names of "Who I am in Christ"*
> *have you already heard?*
> *Where have you put your toddler picture*
> *to remind you of being like a child?*

CHAPTER 8
LEARNING A NEW LANGUAGE

How many languages do you speak well? If you're like most of us, your answer is probably one. Europeans put us to shame. Most of them speak at least two, sometimes four or five. I love languages and I love the way they blend together to form words with nuances beyond the obvious. Because of this linguistic interest I have studied French, Hebrew, German, Latin, and bits of Italian, Greek and Spanish. However, I am not proficient in any of them. I just like to know a little about each one, and the best I can do with any of my more serious attempts is to fairly well navigate my way through a menu or a concordance.

When you begin to study another language, you typically spend time memorizing vocabulary, learning verbal conjugations and noun declensions. If you're not motivated, it can become really difficult. Some of us need to see the written words. Others need to hear the spoken words. Some need both to succeed. But anyone who is really proficient in a language needs to be with someone who speaks it regularly, who converses with them daily, and who expects them to care enough to learn to respond in a meaningful way. Immersion is good.

We go to Europe occasionally for ministry opportunities. Even though we may not know the language of a local country, if we make feeble attempts to converse in their native tongue, we are met with an amazing surge of warmth, help, and incredible hospitality. Just **attempting** to speak in another's native language opens unexpected doors, and amazing graciousness.

Once when we were walking the streets of a small village in Germany, I saw a charming little yarn shop that carried skeins of wool in colors I could never find in the warm southern area where I live. At that time I was having fun knitting purses and felting them. To do this you have to knit with 100% wool, wash it in very hot water and then watch it shrink into the most beautiful dense fabric. Knowing I would never find such an array of colors like this at home, I dragged Conlee into this small shop where two older women were knitting vigorously and drinking coffee. As I looked at the shelves of yarn, they both greeted me warmly, "Guten Tag." I tried very hard to answer them appropriately in German, but the first syllable out of my mouth revealed that I could not speak German. In my feeble attempts to converse with the women and share with them what I wanted yarn for, they (who spoke no English) took a passionate interest in helping me.

First, they offered us coffee, then seats at their table, and then a long and enthusiastic explanation of their wares, helped immensely by much gesturing, pointing, and pictures they pulled out of drawers. It was the most delightful half hour, and I left with several skeins of beautifully dyed yarns and a wealth of good memories. We overcame the language barrier and spoke a common language of interest, respect, passion, and kindness. We actually hugged one another when we walked out of their shop.

The Language of the Heart

Now, let's talk about God's language – the one He speaks to us in intimate ways. It's sometimes called The Language of the Heart. Even though it resonates deep within our being, it's still often a very difficult language to discern – **unless** you are in a heart relationship with the Speaker. [In some ways, it is like speaking with the German ladies. Common interests, respect, and passion pave the way to translation]. God's language is more exquisite than any language on earth. It can contain volumes in one word. It can impart deep healing and affirmation in a single impression. When He speaks to us, it is truly supernatural.

When we receive the great gift of salvation and eternal life from God through His Son Jesus, coming alive spiritually by the power of Holy Spirit within us, we become supernatural creatures, housed temporarily in a natural body. We begin to have the capability of understanding the supernatural language of the Father to whom we belong. We may not be proficient in His language, but we value the Father so much that we will attempt to converse with Him. When we make the slightest effort, He pours out His presence upon us in immeasurable ways.

If you have a relationship with God through Jesus, your Savior, **you have heard Him speak to you!** In some way you heard Him call you, draw you, invite you, bid you come to Him, attract you to Himself.

How did it happen for you?

Everyone hears Him in a different and unique way, but He always finds us and encourages us to follow Him. In the Bible each disciple was called by Jesus in a personal and distinctive way. Some heard His voice directly, some heard about Him through someone else, some saw the wake of His presence (the healings and the changed lives), some heard His preaching and teaching, some who lived many years after His resurrection had a visitation from His Spirit. But one by one, Jesus spoke to hearts in a language each one could receive.

I first "heard" God speak to me by sensing His presence. Many people tell of a warming of the heart or an impression that He is in the midst of difficult circumstances, or a filling of a deep emptiness, or the answer to what they've been looking for. The ways in which He will "speak" to us are limitless, but there is a common theme to all of them. He wants each of us to come closer and closer to Him until He is more important than anything else in our lives. He speaks a language of love, a language that calls your heart to join His.

The heart is something we need to put into Biblical perspective as we talk about "listening with the heart" or the "language of the heart." We moderns tend to think of the "heart" as a place within us that emanates warm, comforting feelings and even pleasing, physical sensations. This is certainly reinforced in our culture by valentines, cupids, and even sayings such as "I ♥ you!" It's no wonder we tend to equate "hearing with the heart" with subjective feelings and sentimentality. But the way in which "heart" is most often used in scripture refers to the "core or center of one's being."

Let's dissect ourselves a bit (not something I recommend

doing, but in this case it may be helpful) according to ancient Greek and Hebrew understandings. Their philosophies under-gird the writers of the Bible.

It was commonly understood that one's intellect, thoughts and concepts come from the mind or the head. That makes sense to us because we associate such activities with the brain.

But the ancients assigned one's emotions, feelings and sentiments (the sensate products of experience) to the region of the bowels. This is more difficult for us to comprehend unless we recall several expressions we commonly use that make reference to this. We speak of having a *feeling in the pit of the stomach,* having *butterflies in the stomach*, or having your *stomach tied up in knots.* Even *gut feeling* implies more of an undefined intuition than a rational, thought-out evaluation. Some newer translations of scripture substitute the words *compassion* or *pity* for the refer-ences to the bowels (i.e. compare 1 John 3:17 in KJV and NIV).

So, Biblically we have the understanding of the head con-taining intellect and the bowels containing emotions or experi-ence. What, then, happens in the heart and why is it mentioned in the Bible so often?

The ancient understanding was that when *intellect* and *emotional experience (feelings)* are combined, they meet in the heart (the core of one's being) and together they form *reason.* Therefore, when I say that I "hear" in my heart, I am assimilat-ing my knowledge about something (intellect) and my experience (feelings) to form reason.

Intellect + Emotional Experience = Reason

Getting out of balance in either the realm of the intellect or the realm of experience and feelings will distort my ability to reason. If I am so heady about God through the kind of theological Bible studies I was in before I was born again, I will never have a reasonable picture of who God is. However, if I rely almost exclusively on whether or not I sense God's presence or feel Him all the time, I am also depriving myself of truly knowing God. He put us together in this mysterious, yet wonderful, tri-part way in which we can discover truth even beyond what we expect.

Here's how I can apply this equation to my initial spiritual awakening. When I first "heard God speak to my heart" I intellectually knew that something was happening way beyond what was expected or what was natural. It was not the norm by anyone's standards. There was a roaring noise; there was an explosion of fire; at the same time there was a holy quiet that settled on all of us. Everyone present was aware of the same things happening. These were facts. They were recounted later and each person confirmed they happened in the same way.

At the same time I was filled with the experience of a holy presence and a super-charged awakening inside me that could not be measured or described in any terms I knew. It was an intuitive sensing but just as real as the physical occurrences.

Putting these two (fact and intuition) together produced the most reasonable and truthful concept I had ever had: I had just been in the presence of the Living God! This truth changed my life.

God created our minds to receive, contain, and impart knowledge. He uses our emotions, feelings, and intuition to bind truths and symbol to our soul. And He brings the two together (intellect and experience) into the heart where we might receive and contain His wisdom.

> *"Come now, let us reason together, says the Lord. Though your sins are like scarlet, they shall be as white as snow; though they are red as crimson, they shall be like wool."*

(Isaiah 1:18)

This scripture is not about God having a conference with sinners to talk them into repentance. He is saying in picturesque language that the very best He has to offer them (the forgiveness of sin and the cleansing of its effects) will be theirs when they accept His perfect blending of truth and experience which is reason.

When we confess our sins, He forgives. That is *intellectual* truth. It is fact.

Then, when He cleanses us from all unrighteousness through His forgiveness, we enjoy the *experience*, the fruit of obedience. (I John 1:9)

Together, this changes the heart! Amazing, isn't it?

We are not accustomed to living our lives from a center of perfect reason. Most of us are out of balance one way or another. Either we tend to be too heady, relying almost exclusively on our intellect and our ability to prove facts and make rational decisions about things. Or conversely, we are living too much out of our feeling-being, constantly seeking experiences to validate truth.

This is why when God speaks into our hearts, so often what we hear surprises us. It is seldom what we expect, yet it is perfect each time. He sets us in balance, giving us a divine order we don't typically have. God goes directly to the heart of a matter – literally. His divine reason can be poured into us in a supernatural way, by-passing our intellectual understanding or our passionate feelings.

In the Bible Jesus spoke into human dilemmas with such perfect reason that the wisest sages were astounded. Remember when He was asked what to do if a woman's husband died and she remarried and who would she be married to in Heaven? (Matthew 22:23-30) Or when a woman was caught in adultery and the authorities just knew that no matter what decision Jesus rendered He would condemn Himself? (John 8:3-11) His answers to their "trick questions" were always perfectly logical, accurate, and in harmony with God's eternal truths. He speaks what the Father puts in His heart. It comes with the perfect assimilation of perfect knowledge and perfect compassion into ultimate reason. This is why we need to hear Him!

In 1972, shortly after I was born again, I read a book by Arthur Katz entitled *Ben Israel, the Odyssey of a Modern Jew.* (Logos International, 1970). In it is an account of Katz' initial encounter with Jesus through His ability to reason perfectly. Katz' testimony impacted me so profoundly that I remember it vividly after all these years.

All his life Art Katz had been searching for truth. He was looking for a deeper meaning to Judaism, an understanding of God, a reason for his existence. He traveled the world, intensely questioning and exploring. Along the way he encountered several people who knew and loved Jesus but he could not understand why. He associated the figure of Jesus with "insipid, weak, wishy-washy, sentimental, submissive" followers. At the age of 34, on December 8, 1963, he was slumped on the steerage deck of a crowded Greek ship, jammed between two Greeks, surrounded by a mixture of humanity, livestock and vats of olive oil. The weather was wild and he looked for a diversion. He remembered a small New Testament that had been distributed to all boarding passengers by the New York Bible Society. Never before having opened the covers of a New Testament, he took it out of his pocket and began to read.

Katz found the book totally different from anything else he had ever read. He was drawn to the man Jesus, not yet knowing who He was, but sensing that He represented everything the world so desperately needed. In Jesus, he saw someone who confronted rather than weakly compromised; who had strength, manliness, keenness of mind, courage, deep insights, compassion and love.

Arthur Katz:

When I came to the episode of a woman taken in adultery (John 8), my pulse quickened as I lived the drama. Here I found a clear-cut case of dispensing justice. The law said that the woman must be stoned. Yet Jesus had been teaching forgiveness, and earlier in the book had actually said, "God sent not his Son into the world to condemn the world, but that the world through Him might be saved." Jesus was trapped. I sensed the relish of those who stood around Him, having ambushed Him into an unanswerable predicament. What could He say?

I closed the book, not wanting to see my new-found hero destroyed. His manliness. His keenness of mind. His courage. His deep insight into life. His compassion and love for the down-trodden. All was to be demolished, it seemed, by a group of self-righteous religionists who had plotted this scheme to get rid of Him because He was threatening their Pharisaic codes of justice and righteousness. My heart actually palpitated, and sweat oozed from the palms of my hands as I fancied the men surrounding Him, their eyes ablaze with hatred and envy, spittle running from their mouths as they gloated over His quandary.

So symbolic, I thought, of the entire human situation as truth comes to grips with selfishness.

What would I say in Jesus' place? I searched my mind, exhausting my resources of logic and reason and finally conceded there was no answer. Fully expecting the worst, I reopened the book and read on. I found Jesus bending over, poking His finger in the dirt. How like me, I thought, stalling for time. Then He looked up, His eyes meeting the eyes of His adversaries. I could see their contorted faces against His quiet control ... His expression – pure, resolute.

"Let him without sin cast the first stone."

I gasped. A sword had been plunged deep into my being. It was numbing, shocking, yet thrilling because the answer was so utterly perfect. It defied cerebral examination. It cut across every major issue I had ever anguished upon in my life. Truth. Justice. Righteousness. Integrity. I knew that what I had read transcended human knowledge and comprehension. It had to be Divine.

In one instant those words leaped off the page and engraved themselves upon my heart. When the shock waves subsided, I sat dumbfounded, realizing that I knew God was – and is. Not a God of our own making. Not a God far away. Not a God who can be contained in the parchments and scrolls of the Ark. Not a God who can be boxed in by institutional religion. But a God who lives.

Ben Israel, Arthur Katz, pages 90-92 [20]

To hear Him more clearly we all need to have healing in our hearts. Damaged emotions, wrong kinds of thinking, pollution from unholy activities, etc., will cloud the heart's ability to rightly discern what God is saying. It is impossible to encourage you to hear with your heart and not also encourage you to let God heal your heart. We'll be doing some of that as we go along.

The language of the heart is conveyed to us in a much more mysterious way than cognitive thinking. Cognitive thought can be argued, analyzed, doubted, proven or disproven. Yet the way the heart is made aware of truth is greatly influenced by intuition. Therefore, the language of the heart is difficult to defend. It is more a matter of trust than proof. It involves an inner knowing that may be so slight and fleeting at times it is easy to miss.

Just as we are told to submit our minds to God so that we can be renewed in our thinking,[21] we must also submit our intuitive faculties to Him so we can recognize how He speaks to us. Many people will have great difficulty trusting in their intuitive faculties (or those of others) until they learn to surrender them to God. But equally as important, those people who are more comfortable with intuitive ways of reasoning must also submit themselves to God, so that their own intuition has healthy boundaries.

---

20   Arthur Katz committed his life to serving Jesus after his conversion. He went from being a self-proclaimed Marxist/atheist to leading Art Katz Ministries, traveling the world to tell of the life-changing power of serving Jesus Christ. He died July 28, 2007, at the age of 78.

21   Romans 12:2

When considering how you rely on either your mind (intellect and measureable facts) or your emotions (feelings and intuition), are you out of balance in either direction?

Has this affected your ability to hear and employ God's wisdom as you reason through a situation?

Write this in your Listening Prayer Journal and have a conversation with God about it.

CHAPTER 9

ONE GOD WHO SPEAKS
IN MANY WAYS

In an Audible Voice and Through The Bible

Before we make the language of the heart seem too difficult or too theoretical to put into practice, we will look at some of the various ways God may speak to us. Keep in mind that many of these ways may be very subtle and may overlap. This list is not exhaustive. I've not included receiving from angels, seeing God's handwriting on tablets of stone or on a wall, visions, pictures, or music. These are all Biblical, and there are many more. Perhaps, you will want to add to my list after the following chapters.

- *An Audible voice*

    I'm starting with this one so we can get it out of the way, because it really doesn't require heart language at all. Of course, we'd all love to have a clear, oral, spoken channel from God. If we were able to tune in at will, like turning the dial on a radio, we wouldn't have to change our life-style very much to hear Him. We could even do other things (multi-task) while carrying on a conversation with Him. We do that with humans all the time. We become accustomed to listening to someone with one ear, the TV with the other, darting our eyes around to see what else is going on, and using both hands on a task, all at the same time. We even define this activity as something of value: efficiency. I've already mentioned that one of my all-time pet peeves is to be attempting to have a personal conversation with someone while they are texting on a cell phone. I understand that they really think they can pay attention to both at once but I consider their lack of attention to be inconsiderate, rude and demeaning. It's the same reason why I don't ever ask someone on the phone to hold while I answer another call. It's like saying to the person on the phone, "Wait a minute, someone more important to me than you might be calling me." And yet, we do this with God all the time!

Efficient multi-tasking may produce results in the world, but it doesn't work so well in the Spirit realm. God made us spiritual creatures and learning to hear His Spiritual voice is a good way to live into our destined identity.

Several people I know have actually heard God speak audibly. At our conferences we often ask how many have heard Him this way and there are always a few hands that go up. Yet, I have never met anyone who says this is the way God regularly speaks to them. It is an out-of-the-ordinary experience to get their attention. This has never happened to me but it profoundly changed my mother when she heard Him speak out loud.

After a lifetime of resisting Him and several years of arguing with me about her fears of my having a personal relationship with Jesus, in her sixties my mother audibly heard God call her name and tell her to go back to the church of her youth. Home alone, she was so startled by the authoritative, masculine voice that she turned over a can of green paint on the back patio where she was painting lawn chairs. That green stain on the flagstone remains tangible proof to this day of an experience that led to her becoming born of the Spirit. She never heard Him speak audibly again, but He got her attention in an undeniable way and put her on a road that brought her into His healing love. He changed her life! All my years of arguing with her, defending myself, and bombarding her with books and tapes were for naught. That one audible voice she heard on a spring morning did what I could never do.

So, I believe with all my heart that God does speak audibly sometimes; I saw the evidence in my family. He certainly did it Biblically. But when we receive His Spirit, it is much more usual for us to hear from the heart. The Spirit in us equips us for this heart-listening.

We don't need to spend much time on this topic because expecting God to speak regularly to you in this way will be frustrating. If it does happen to you, give thanks to God, write what He says in your Listening Prayer Journal, and ask Him to show you what to do with the word He gives. He will be encouraging you to hear with your heart, not with your auditory faculties.

• *The Bible*

Doing anything the exact same way for long periods of times gets monotonous. Eating the same food, wearing the same clothes, driving the same route, etc. Don't panic now when I say this, but reading the Bible can get monotonous as well. This says nothing negative about the Bible. It says a lot about human nature.

At our conferences we always have a time on the first night to minister to people who have grown stale in their passion for the Word of God. You wouldn't believe how they stream forward! And these are pastors, Sunday School teachers, Bible teachers, missionaries, as well as lay people. At first they are a little embarrassed to admit it. I've been embarrassed to admit it! Christians aren't supposed to get tired of the Bible. But, when we confess the truth, and pray for a new passion for God's Word, we find this is certainly a prayer He loves to answer! Maybe He's just waiting for us to ask?

> *Lord, would You give me a new passion for Your Word today?*
> *Would You set my heart on fire as I read Your Word?*
> *Would You help me discover You in new ways*
> *through Your Word?*

What is the purpose of the Bible? Unfortunately, many believers use it only as a study book or a proof text. Yes, you can study it for a life-time and not begin to discover all the complexities and intricate, multi-faceted nuances and meanings. It is limitless because it is inspired by God. And we need to study it, to learn, to establish that Divine Plumb Line in our lives. It is vital!

But what if you also begin to look at the Bible as the vehicle God uses to reveal His character and His deep love to YOU? How easy it is to forget to read the Word personally!

Daily devotionals are great. I've written many of them, and I also read one every morning. However, think about what you are doing when you read your devotional page each day. Yes, you are taking in the Word, but then you are allowing someone else to interpret if for you and apply it to your life. That's a lot easier and quicker than sitting quietly, waiting for God to interpret the Word to your heart - but it's certainly not as personal.

On most social networks on the internet there are people who are doing the 365x journals, posting a personal picture and writing a sentence or two from their life each day for a year. For a while I was even receiving through email an original painting a day from a local artist! This daily activity is also trendy among bloggers. But, once again, God had the idea first! He says to us: *"Blessed is the one who listens to Me, watching at My doors day by day, waiting beside My doorway."* (Proverbs 8:34)

As you come to His door waiting for Him each day, open the Book He has given you and ask Him to show you within its covers another living testament of His love for you. Let Him guide you to the scripture for the day. Or, if you're using another guide for a daily reading, ask Him specifically to speak to you through what you read. And continue to pray: *Lord, give me a passion for Your Word that is greater than what I have had before. Set my heart on fire for You and Your Word today. Burn Your truth into my life. I want to come closer to You.*

Here are several interesting things you can choose to do when you read the Word. They may be new to you. I suggest you give them a try so that your time in the Word of God will be an exciting and rewarding experience:

- *Read until God brings a portion alive for you or gives you an impression that this is important for you today. Then Stop! Look! Listen!*

- *Take any passage that God highlights for you and write it out in your Journal, substituting personal pronouns. Hear Him saying it just to you!*

- *Go through the Gospels, writing out each command from Jesus. Insert your name in each one and allow Him to write them on your heart as well as in your mind.*

- *Read just the red-lettered words in the New Testament. Stop to listen at regular intervals!*

- *Put yourself in the story you read. Where are you? How are you reacting to the situation? Which person do you most identify with? Which one is hard to identify with? What is the Lord saying to you?*

CHAPTER 10

ONE GOD WHO SPEAKS
IN MANY WAYS

Through Dreams, Sermons, Teachings, and Books

* *Dreams*

Have you ever had such an intense dream that you woke up with your heart pounding and the certainty that it was really important? Chances are that if you didn't write it down you won't remember the details of it today. It's always a good idea to record your dreams in your Listening Prayer Journal. Dreams have the capacity to contain volumes of truth in a few seconds of symbolic pictures. They are worth paying attention to. If you don't write them out immediately, they will vanish like a cloud.

Many years ago Conlee and I, both skeptical about how God would speak to us in dreams, made a decision to try a little experiment during a two week vacation. We vowed to pray each night before bed, asking God to speak to us in dreams and to help us remember them the next morning. We promised Him we would write whatever we dreamed in our Journals without analyzing or trying to interpret them.

Conlee was pretty sure his dreams, if he had any at all, were going to reflect what he had eaten the night before, but he was willing to give it a try. Sure enough, every morning we both had the memories of vivid dreams to write out. At first they made no sense at all and seemed disjointed, but we faithfully record- ed them without trying to translate them into something that seemed logical.

At the end of the two weeks we shared the compilation of dreams with one another and we were amazed. Each of us saw a definite pattern woven throughout our individual series of dreams. It was helpful for us to share them with one another. Then they became less subjective and we could see patterns much easier. The circumstances in each dream were different, but the basic themes were the same. What we learned from God during that period of time was very instrumental in shaping our future, preparing us both for something we were not anticipating. For us, although we didn't know it at the time, it was full-time minis- try.

There are so many books written about dreams and dream interpretations. One popular theory is that there are universal symbols in dreams that mean the same thing to all people.[22] For instance, dreaming of fire would always symbolize a passion, or dreaming of water would always symbolize a cleansing, etc. I think this is a cop-out. If you buy into this theory, then when

22   There is no Biblical basis for this theory. Rather, universal dream symbolic systems are compiled by anthropologists, psychologists, and metaphysicists who differ widely on their interpretations.

you have a dream you don't understand, all you have to do is look up all the symbolic components in a dream guide and fill in the blanks. It precludes listening to God and letting Him interpret the symbols for you. It's somewhat like having your spouse speak intimate loving words to you that convey deep love and concern, but instead of your responding, you go tell an acquaintance about it and ask your friend to tell you what your spouse meant. Not very personal, is it? And, it leaves the interpretation wide open to distort genuine intentions.

Besides losing the personal aspect of the dream conversation with God, a universal symbolic system can border on the same principle as horoscopes and astrology. It is allowing someone else to plant images into your mind and heart and guide your life. The Bible calls this witchcraft.

I told you that I sometimes like to use a loose leaf binder for my Listening Prayer Journal so that I can index sections of it for specific purposes. One of those sections is for recording dreams. It is helpful for me to date the dream and leave space underneath to write later after God reveals the meaning to me.

On Christmas Day, 2007, I dreamed I walked into my closet and on two shelves in a little alcove there were eight babies, four on each shelf. That was all there was to it. It was very vivid. I wrote it down and dated it. Later, asking God to show me what this meant, He spoke to me in my heart and told me I would have another grandchild. We already had seven grandchildren. Nothing happened, no announcements. But, in June of 2011, our oldest son (who always insisted they would have no children), happily married and in his late forties, announced they were expecting their first child! Of course, everyone was ecstatic and very surprised. I photographed my Journal entry and sent it to them. God knew this child before he was conceived in his mother's womb. (Jeremiah 1:5a) I think the dream was more for my son and daughter-in-law (and for their son, Graham, one day) than for me. But it was exactly the kind of conversation a loving God would share with His beloved child. It was like He wanted to tell me the good news first because He loves me!

I have many dreams in my Journal for which I have not yet received a full meaning. But I have not lost them. They are alive because they are recorded, and one day God will reveal to me what is now hidden. I believe He continues to give me dreams because I cherish them and thank Him for them, both those I understand and those I don't.

- *Sermons / Teachings / Books*

I'm combining these three categories, although each could stand on its own. But collectively, these are ways we can hear God through the applications other people give to what they have heard and studied. It's very easy for us to rely exclusively upon these ways of hearing God. We don't have to spend the intensive time of preparation, do the homework, the study, or change our routine very much. We just get to enjoy the fruits of others.

Obviously, some sermons are anointed, bringing the true word of God and transforming lives, and some are merely man's wisdom and not so helpful. Some are merely entertaining. Some are inspiring and some are a little ho-hum. But hearing God through a sermon is often a "jumping-off" place for us. You may hear what a preacher is saying but at the same time God might take you somewhere else, or deeper into the subject, or make a personal connection with you, or impress a truth into your heart.

It is really exciting when this happens.

You may personally "hear" something in a sermon that no one else in the congregation hears. It is a way that God, knowing all your circumstances, will use the preacher's words to speak just to you, even though the preacher may intend a totally different application. Conlee says that often a person will greet him at the end of a church service to thank him for a sermon that spoke to his heart. When he asks the person, "What was it that God used in the sermon to speak to you?" the person often tells him about something Conlee had not said at all, perhaps not even thought about. But God used the sermon to direct that person to His agenda for them. When that happens to any of us, we may tend to give the credit to the preacher, calling him a great man of God, rather than praising God for His personal word.

A good preacher should be a messenger from God to you. He is not called by God to entertain or to put on a big production. His obligation is to listen to what God is saying and to impart it to the people. He points the people to God, not to himself, and he encourages them to hear God personally and come closer to His heart. Delivering a sermon is a high calling and a huge responsibility.

Some of the more dynamic, flamboyant preaching personalities that we tend to admire can only get in the way of the impartation of God's word. There are many cultural aspects to preaching. Some congregations like shouters; some prefer a reserved person who is quiet and restrained. Some people prefer a preacher who walks all over the room; others want someone who stands behind a pulpit. The style we prefer is mainly what we get used to. But none of these outward appearances or styles determines the way God may speak to you through a sermon. The criteria for you to hear God in a sermon is not dependent on the preacher's delivery, but whether or not the preacher has heard from God and is willing to stay true to God's Word.

How do you define a "good sermon?" My definition is one in which God continues to speak to me long after the service is over. Of course, this involves deliberate reflection about it on my part. I must take it seriously and apply it personally. I want to be assured that the preacher is in an active, personal relationship with God, and is listening to God on a regular basis. I want to hear what God has been saying to the preacher recently rather than what he just read in a book. I expect the words of the preacher to line up with scripture and to bring me closer to Jesus. I want the sermon to make a difference in my life.

As you can tell, I have very high standards for sermons and church services. It's a challenge to keep these high standards and yet not be critical when they are not realized. But, I don't want to go to church to be entertained, to hear book reports, or to receive a "new revelation." I want to be in the presence of God with other believers to worship freely and authentically, to be exhorted, challenged and encouraged by the Word of God, and to be in an environment that allows God to move in our midst as He wills.

Delivering a life-changing sermon week after week is a tall order. Married to a man who was the active pastor of a church for twenty years, I can tell you that not every Sunday is a "home-run." Very few pastors are exclusively "preaching pastors." Most of them have a myriad of other responsibilities to the congregation all week. Crises in the congregation, in one's family, and many other circumstances often disrupt planned, quiet, listening-to-God times for any pastor. But, the point of hearing God through a sermon is not whether or not the preacher "nailed it" every time; it's what I allow God to do with it.

> *In church each week: am I listening to God*
> *as well as to the preacher?*
> *Do I continue to reflect on the Sunday words*
> *during the rest of the week?*
> *Am I asking God questions about the sermon?*
> *Am I doing further study about what I heard?*
> *Am I talking with others about the subject?*

Am I allowing a sermon to die a premature death when the service is over, or am I allowing it to live, breathe, and marinate in me as I bring it to my own quiet time? Interestingly, some of the most ordinary, unimaginative sermons can turn into life-changing messages for me when I invite God into a dialogue about them.

There are hundreds of sermons available at any given time on the internet. Archives of church services around the world are just waiting to be watched and heard. Because of the vast difference between HUMAN TIME ZONE and GOD TIME ZONE, God can easily speak to us clearly and relevantly through all kinds of media. The power of God can move with great might through the technology of the computer, the recording, the radio, the TV, and the printed page. Through any of them He can, and often does, speak a relevant word to hearts that are listening, and bring them salvation and healing for the soul and body. That one word that comes from God to me will be of more value than the finest sermon ever preached.

In my indexed Journal I have a section for Sermon Notes.

It helps me tremendously to listen in church with my Journal and pen in hand (or, I confess- iPad!), often balancing a Bible as well. Jotting down scripture references and cryptic notes about what God is saying to me about the subject is very helpful in the days to come as I reflect on the message. Even my notes provide further jumping-off places for God to speak to me.

If you haven't tried simple note-taking during sermons, give it a try.

Teachings and books, while amazing vehicles for God's words to enter His people, can also become substitutes for hearing God's voice for ourselves. We can follow a teacher or a writer, just like a preacher, to the extent that we let them "listen for us." Sometimes we quote them more than God Himself. Allowing good sermons, teachings and books to be starting lines rather than finish lines, puts them in perspective in our lives. The point of any of these God-given blessings is to point us to the intimate relationship with God that He desires.

At our *Journey to Wholeness in Christ* conferences our primary goal is to see an intimacy with God increased in the life of each participant. If a participant goes home from our conference just quoting to others what we taught, or analyzing the material they received, Conlee and I have failed in our mission. But, when we hear later testimonies that, after a *Journey* conference, one's marriage improved, or one is excited in a fresh way about getting into the Bible, or one's depression has lifted, or one is becoming active in a ministry, then we rejoice that true intimacy with Jesus has been renewed and He is continuing to bring wholeness.

At our conferences and at other Christian conferences, most people come bearing tote bags or back packs carrying supplies to take copious notes of lectures. They would love (and often ask for) handouts and even a syllabus but we don't give them either. Sometimes we even ask them to put away all their notes and close their eyes so they can clearly hear God. Many people have never learned to do this.

Although we have our books, CDs and DVDs available at every conference, our objective is not to fill their heads with more information, but to provide an environment for God to do His transforming work. We deliberately provide time for ministry with each subject that is presented. Learning this rhythm of:

> ➢ taking in knowledge,
> ➢ allowing God to translate it into your life, and then
> ➢ listening to what He says to you about it

is as valuable a lesson as anything taught at a conference. You may have to attend a conference to learn to do this, but bringing the practice home with you afterwards will be life-changing.

In my Journal there is also a section to jot down notes from books I am reading. I often learn as much from the footnotes as I do from the texts of books. I love to know what the author has read, what has been the inspiration. Buying one good book often leads to three or four more if God uses it in my life.

I tend to read topically and then move right into serendipity. That is, I will begin with an author such as Abraham Heschel and read everything I can find that he has written. Then, often I will begin with another author Heschel mentions and exhaust his writings, and on and on. Or, a friend will give me a highly-recommended book and the footnotes and references in it start me off on another adventure, following the trails God opens up.

I also mark up books without hesitation. These are not expensive collections. They are books to be enjoyed, referenced, turned-down, and written in the margins. One of my most valued possessions is a Bible that belonged to my great-great-grandfather. In the margins are all kinds of notes written in his formal penmanship. He wrote everything from what kind of weather they had the day he was reading a certain verse to where he was going, to a lesson he learned from the scripture. Although I never met him, I love the personal connection he and I have down through the ages. I also buy used books whenever possible for this same reason. Margin notes and underlined passages from previous owners delight me. Plus, I save a lot of money!

You can tell that I love to read, and I have since childhood. Yet, as much as it pleases me, it cannot compare with hearing a personal word from God. Sometimes in the midst of my reading time, I will just stop, close my eyes and let Him speak to my heart. It may be about what I just read or something entirely different. Reading stimulates my mind but it also quiets my body and readies my heart to receive. I just have to keep my priorities in order and **not** let myself say, "Just a minute, Lord. I have to finish this chapter."

CHAPTER 11

ONE GOD WHO SPEAKS IN MANY WAYS

Through Worship

- *Worship*

Worship styles are as varied as people are. Oh, my goodness!

We worship with our words, sometimes in silence, sometimes shouting, sometimes collectively with liturgy, sometimes spontaneously, sometimes in the Spirit.

We worship with our body, sometimes kneeling, sometimes on our faces, sometimes standing with hands raised, sometimes walking or marching, sometimes dancing, sometimes yielded to His power.

We worship with music, sometimes Gospel, sometimes Christian country, sometimes Gregorian chant, sometimes contemporary Christian with drums and screaming guitars, sometimes traditional hymns, sometimes classical sacred.

> *What else can you think of?*
> *What manner of worship draws you closest to God?*
> *What physical posture enhances worship for you?*
> *Do you worship God most freely out loud or quietly?*
> *What are your favorite worship songs? Why?*
> *Consider trying a style you've never experienced before.*
> *See what happens!*

Most likely the worship songs you like best are the ones through which you have sensed the presence of God. When you hear them or sing them, they evoke a meaningful time from your past when God was very real to you. At most of our *Journey* conferences Kirk and Deby Dearman lead worship. They have ministered with us since 1992, and the *Journey* ministry is in their hearts. They know it well and they have experienced much healing. At a *Journey*, worship is far more than some opening songs, "call-back" music, and background for ministry times. We see God move powerfully in people when they genuinely worship.

Kirk and Deby often write songs that reflect our teachings and point people to God to receive what they just heard taught. Therefore, worship is woven throughout every teaching and is an integral part of all personal ministry. Because of this, when people go home from such a conference and play a CD of the music that ministered so powerfully to them, they are caught up once more in the presence of God and receive further healing each time they hear one of the Dearman's songs like "The Cross is the Place for My Pain," or "I Choose to Forgive," or "Draw Me Jesus."

Worship music can be either vertical or horizontal. Horizontal worship is just what it sounds like. It is music **about** God or how you feel about God that is played and sung to gather people together, to perform, to entertain, and/or to make the artists sound and look good.

Vertical worship is offered up **to** God. When a worship leader is truly worshiping rather than performing, the people worship as well. This kind of worship can take one right into the intimate presence of God where He speaks, heals, and saves. I have received physical healings during such worship without anyone specifically praying for me. Vertical worship is a powerful vehicle to take us out of ourselves and upwards to Him.

Ruth Heflin wrote in her book, *Glory*,[23] the following exhortation for entering into the presence of God where healing and miracles occur:

> *Praise ...until the Spirit of worship comes.*
> *Worship ... until the glory comes.*
> *Then ... stand in the glory.*

I first read her book years ago, liked it very much, and then put it on a shelf. It was not until recently that the Lord reminded me of the truth of this simple blueprint for entering into God's presence. I asked the Lord to show me how this works for a group of people such as those who come to our conferences. He gave me a vivid image of a room full of people sitting quietly, waiting for us to begin our first session. Some were expectant, some were nervous, others scared. This is typical of a first night at a *Journey*. In this picture from God we began with praise and worship

---

23   Heflin, Ruth Ward, Glory, The McDougal Publishing Co, Hagerstown, MD, 1990.

music as we usually do. Some stood, some sang, some looked around, some never opened their mouths. Again, typical. Then God showed me something I had never seen before; it was an instructed worship session. He said to me, *I want you to do this!*

Unless I was absolutely sure God showed me what to do and told me to do it, I would never have done what I did at our next conference. I followed His scenario to the letter, letting Him lead me as to timing and choreography. First, as I already mentioned, we put NO PASSIVITY ZONE posters on the doors and the announcement was made about the serious intention to move out of our passive attitudes. It was not a "scolding" so much as a "heads-up" that all of us were going to be aware anytime we slipped back to our default position. Then I prayed aloud that God would remind us and energize us to be "disturbed" by His Spirit. Although, this was very different, they seemed to take it all pretty well.

The next thing God led me to do was to call upon the Spirit of worship to descend upon us. I invited each person to begin by praising God for who He is and what He does. I explained that praise is not the same as worship. Praise is an awareness of those around you, all joining in together to sing about or to extol God's greatness. Praise gives honor to God and is a genuine expression of what is in our hearts. Praise moves us into worship.

Worship is the attitude of the heart that becomes absorbed in who God is, where He is, what He is saying, and how I am in relationship with Him. It is extremely intimate and personal. Each person will experience worship differently and should respond whole-heartedly.

I continued to do what God instructed. I asked the people,

as they praised God, to get out of their row, come to the aisle, and make their way down to the front as soon as they experienced the slightest awareness of entering into a more intimate realm with the Lord, the realm of worship. I asked them to be aware when their focus changed. All the while Kirk and Deby were leading us in songs of love **to** Jesus, not **about** Jesus. This was so new to most of us that everyone was hesitant at first. We're not accustomed to having someone instruct us in worship. *We want to do it ourselves!* But we were all learning God's way and what pleases Him. And this was a very cooperative group!

It took a long time for people to respond to God, to actually leave their comfortable nests they had already prepared, and come forward. I waited. I kept saying, *God, are you sure? What if no one comes forward?* But God gave me such a sweet peace and assurance that this was what He wanted to do. I was to trust and wait. We must have gone through three or four songs before a man in the center section crawled over everyone on his row and made his way to the aisle. He stood there alone for a while, obviously lost in worship. Then others began to join him, filling the aisles. When several people began to genuinely worship, it became easier for others to enter into the Spirit of worship we had asked God to give. Worship births deeper worship!

Then I instructed them as God showed me, to walk to the front to enter into His glory where miracles occur. We were in a liturgical church with an altar rail which led to steps to a higher level where the altar table for communion stood. Normally, in this denomination this is the area where the priests, pastors, and other leaders stand. Lay people seldom go "inside the rail." But as soon as the invitation was given, everyone who was standing moved inside the rail around the communion table. From that time on, it became apparent that God was leading them, not me. Some knelt, some fell prostrate on the floor, each one (especially me!) was in awe of the presence of God. Many men and women were weeping.

God then told me to offer an invitation to those remaining in their rows, "If you need a miracle in your life, come join these who are in the glory." Everyone else streamed forward. They were packed in. The Spirit of worship had come. We were doing it God's way and He opened the windows of heaven. This was the conference where there were so many physical healings as well as emotional healings.

Watching in wonder at what had transpired in about an hour's time, I was filled with several impressions:

- When we obey God, even if it is risky, we see Him move in awesome ways.
- The move of God has nothing to do with eloquent preaching, brilliant teaching, or exceptional music. He comes when we seek Him with all our heart, soul, mind and strength.
- What had become a traditional symbolic barrier between the unholy and the holy (the rail that separated lay and clergy) was non-existent when the Spirit of God was in control. It was "the veil being rent."
- As everyone gathered around the communion table, the altar, we were all truly receiving Holy Communion. We were personally partaking of the spiritual Body and Blood of our Lord Jesus Christ, yet no physical elements such as bread and wine were involved.
- In the glory of God anything is possible.
- When I get out of the way, surrender my plans and agenda, and just do what God shows me to do, He does great and un-

expected things.

- The only thing risky for me about obeying God in unusual circumstances is putting my own reputation on the line. I never risk His reputation. Once I actually began to follow His instructions, I cared very little about what people thought of me. Obeying God places the focus on Him and not on the opinions of others.

We most often think of worship in a music category. And it's a wonderful category! But let's think about worship as **your personal offering to God.** If you go to any Bible concordance and look up "worship" you can get excited just reading the many verses about it. My computer concordance lists 1045 verses specifically describing worship. In the dictionary words such as "adoration," "honor," "reverence," and "extravagant love" define worship. These descriptions imply that I, the worshiper, am giving something very special to the One I worship. Something I don't give to anyone else. Something that is so special and so deliberate that it is extremely intimate. It describes a personal encounter with the One I worship. In the church we attend now even giving a monetary offering is a personal, joyful, heartfelt worship to God!

In such encounters I am open and vulnerable to hear whatever God, the object of my worship, says to me. My words and acts of worship are never to bribe Him, but rather are an invitation to engage in dialogue with Him. If it ever becomes routine, it ceases to be worship. If it ever becomes a means to an end, it ceases to be worship. I worship Him because I love Him – for no other reason!

When this happened at the conference I described, people afterwards were filled with an intense passion and love for God that extended to their interactions with those around them. There was an unusual openness to prayer and ministry the rest of the weekend. What God revealed to me through speaking to my heart, and then demonstrated through opening windows of Glory to His people, has changed me and changed the way I minister.

When Paul urges us to,*"offer your bodies as living sacrifices, holy and pleasing to God – this is your reasonable (or spiritual) act of worship,"*[24] he is describing the kind of vertical worship that draws us into God's presence. This is the perfect blending of the intellect and the emotions coming together in the heart as "reasonable" which is spiritual worship. Our whole person worships. This includes the body posture, the voice, the will, and all the senses.

Leading a worship service is a high calling from God. He uses pastors to lead the people into that vertical position where each one present can respond to whatever God wants to do. Recently I heard a pastor describe what it is like to collaborate with Holy Spirit to minister to the people in his congregation at any given service. He said every service has some moment, often coming unexpectedly, when the Spirit opens a window of opportunity He wants to move through. The window may be as small as a peep-hole or as large as a picture window. But the minister's obligation is to put aside anything else that was planned so that God can do whatever He wants.

This takes a total commitment to obey God on the part of the minister. It takes a person who knows how to recognize God's voice when He speaks, and one who is not so married to tradition

---

24   Romans 12:1

that he won't yield to the movement of the Spirit. It takes a person who values the move of God more than delivering the sermon he spent days preparing. That's why being a pastor, a preacher, or a minister is such a holy calling, more than just another job, more than a prestigious identity in the community, but a true ordination and anointing for God's purposes.

When we worship at home, or anywhere else besides church, there is no less commitment to listening and responding to God's opportunities to enter into His presence. The window of opportunity to enter into intimate worship may come in the middle of a sentence you are reading, through a thought in prayer, or even while doing a mundane task. It is your responsibility to respond, to focus on the Lord, to set aside your agenda. Worship moves you into His presence. Worship changes you. Worship opens windows to Heaven and God's Glory. Worship releases the power of Holy Spirit.

Ask God for a Spirit of worship!

CHAPTER 12

ONE GOD WHO SPEAKS IN MANY WAYS

Through Prophecy

- *Prophets*

        I want to spend quite a bit of time on the role of the prophet in hearing God. It can be a confusing subject, open to lots of different ideas and teachings. Only after I deliberately began asking God to instruct me about this gift did I begin to have a deep appreciation for it and to receive increased blessings from prophets used by God. Much of my confusion came from bad experiences combined with fearful teachings. I asked God to sort them out and when He did, I renounced what was not of Him.

        Biblically, a prophet is a person who listens to God, hears a word from Him, and delivers it when, where, and how God directs. However, it's helpful to distinguish between the *calling of a prophet* and the *gift of prophecy*.

THE CALLING OF A PROPHET: There is a divine supernatural dimension to be called to the office of prophet. Paul lists the appointment of prophet among the primary callings of God for the church: apostles, prophets, evangelists, pastors and teachers.[25] Most often this calling comes in one's childhood and may be evident even before the person is born again. Often it is a calling that is misunderstood for years and eventually is confirmed only after many struggles and much spiritual warfare. This is because the prophet's life is so completely different from what the world accepts as a standard for living and relating to God and others. Also, there is often warfare in a prophet's life because the office of prophet is designed by God to reveal and destroy the kingdom of darkness.

A prophet may mishandle his/her calling and even abuse it until it is submitted to God and refined by Him. When one's call is established, the ability to discern spirits and the spiritual climate of situations becomes so much a part of a prophet's identity it seems to be natural to him. Without striving to listen, the one called to be a prophet is so tuned in to the spiritual realm that he just knows when something is real, without any proof or logical explanation. In fact, it seems so real, he can be frustrated with others who cannot discern the same things.

This profile of prophets is supernatural in its characteristics. God pours something extraordinary into these men and women and He uses them in extraordinary ways. Prophets sometimes get the reputation of being odd, super-charged people of God who seem to read His mail and deliver flaming warnings to others. Quite a few seem to live up to this persona. But the outward appearance and the style of delivery do not define a

---

25   Ephesians 4:11

prophet.

A true prophet knows how to discern the presence of God, and allows God's identity to be his own. A prophet hears God and responds, knowing that God's words for an individual or for a people are always redemptive. No matter how strong a warning may be, or how uncomfortable a prophet's words may make some people, God's ultimate goal is to bring wholeness and abundant life to those who have ears to hear.

For some who are unusually gifted in the prophetic, they become so filled with God's word they can't keep quiet even if they try. The Old Testament prophet Jeremiah had this profound kind of calling. He heard from God so clearly and spoke what God told him so obediently that he was scorned by people all around him. The words that God gave him were strong warnings against sin and rebellion and coming disaster if they didn't repent. The people didn't want to hear it and blamed the messenger. At one point Jeremiah lamented,

"I am ridiculed all day long; everyone mocks me. Whenever I speak, I cry out proclaiming violence and destruction. So (speaking) the word of the Lord has brought me insult and reproach all day long." [26]

At this point Jeremiah must have decided that he didn't want to be a prophet anymore. In fact, he determined that he was never going to speak another word God gave him.

"But if I say, 'I will not mention Him or speak any more in His name,' His word is in my heart like a fire, a fire shut up in

---

26   Jeremiah 20:7b-8

my bones. I am weary of holding it in; indeed, I cannot." [27]

I have known a few men and women with this kind of supernatural calling. They paid a price for yielding to the calling, but each would say that the rewards far surpassed what they sacrificed. From childhood they knew they were different. They always had a strong inner drawing to spiritual things. Most of them struggled with unholy spirits until they totally submitted their calling to God. Evil spirits want to thwart the work of God and want to twist God's gifts and use them for their own purposes.

Prophets tend to be impatient with those who do not "hear" or "see" in the Spirit realm as easily or quickly. When their gift is under submission to God, they "know" things hidden to most of us, without needing proof or confirmation from others. Their difficulty is often what to do with the knowledge they receive.

The true prophets whom I know personally are frequently criticized even within the church; they are laughed at, labeled as being divisive, and publicly ostracized by some. I even know of one instance where the adult son of a prophet was hit and knocked down in the church foyer by a lay leader, all because of something his father had proclaimed that he had heard from God!

On the other hand, these same people are loved and honored, extolled, and perhaps even lifted up by their admirers as such exemplary Christians that the amount of admiration poured out on them can become unhealthy.

True prophets are polarizing and they are lightning rods.

---

27   Jeremiah 20:9

> *Who are the men and women with such a prophetic*
> *calling who are speaking out today?*
> *What are they saying?*
> *How are they received by Christians?*
> *How are they received by non-Christians?*
> *Pray for those with such a prophetic calling!*

If this is your calling I would be very surprised if you are reading this book. True prophets just hear God without striving. They don't know any other way to relate to Him but to be aware of what He is saying. They don't need to **practice** hearing Him. They just do it. They are constantly aware of what He is showing them.

THE GIFT OF PROPHECY: This book is for the rest of us. We may not be called to the office of prophet, but we are called, as all Christians are, to prophesy. Paul says,

"Follow the way of love and eagerly desire spiritual gifts, especially the gift of prophecy."[28]

Prophecy is a spiritual gift God gives to the church – all the church. He gives it to you! And like any of the other gifts God gives us, it should be submitted to spiritual authority. For me, this means having a trusted pastor or spiritually mature prayer partner from whom I am willing to receive exhortation and correction when necessary. Unless I am willing to do this, I know I

---

28   1 Corinthians 14:1

should not be trusted to exercise God's gifts.

So, how does this *gift of prophecy* that we all are to desire differ from the more radical call of being a prophet? The subject can become confusing without examining the scriptures closely and also lifting up to God some of the ingrained ideas we have assumed or been wrongly taught.

Paul addresses the *gift of prophecy* quite a bit to Christians in Corinth. He says,

"Everyone who prophesies speaks to men for their strengthening, encouragement and comfort."[29]

He emphasizes that when people listen to God, hear a word from Him, and then speak it to others as directed, they participate in a ministry of strengthening, encouraging, and comforting the Body of Christ. He says,

"I would like every one of you to speak in tongues, but I would rather have you prophesy. He who prophesies is greater than one who speaks in tongues, unless he interprets, so that the church may be edified." [30]

He is saying that when a person hears a message from God and shares it as God directs, the church is strengthened. This is because God's word to us brings life and wholeness.

Paul encourages each believer to *be eager to prophesy*[31] yet realizes that *you will not know perfectly* every word from

---

29   1 Corinthians 14:3
30   1 Corinthians 14:4-5
31   1 Corinthians 14:39

God because of your humanity,[32] and that whatever you receive from God and then share with someone, *must be saturated in love.*[33] When you think about these excellent admonitions and apply them to yourself and the way you converse with others it is so practical and so profoundly helpful. What if everything we shared with others was covered by the same carefully thought out plan for living that Paul gave the Corinthians? We would be:

- Listening more carefully to what God is saying
- Praying more earnestly about what we speak to others
- Speaking in great humility and love, knowing that our wisdom is not infinite.

In this sense, if you are filled with God's Spirit, you have the ability to hear His voice, to receive His directions and live in a prophetic way. This is God's gift to you and to all believers. This is a way I want to live every day. In this sense **we all are able to prophesy.**

We meet regularly with a group of like-minded people who pray for one another that we will keep this goal foremost in our lives. We attempt to hold one another accountable and en-courage and bless one another in this prophetic way of living. We realize that God will use us when we yield ourselves to Him, to sometimes speak a strong prophetic word into someone's life as He directs. This encourages us to listen attentively to God. We realize also that when we yield ourselves to Him, He will open opportunities for a prophetic voice to go forth from us often when we are not even aware of it happening.

_____ I was checking out my fresh fruit and vegetables one day

32   1 Corinthians 13:9
33   1 Corinthians 13:2

at our local curb market. The young woman at the cash register looked so worried that it was the most natural thing in the world for me to say to her, "I hope you know that there is nothing so serious that God's love will not cover you and bring healing."

Astonished, she said, "How did you know?"

"Know what?" I asked.

"Know that my brother-in-law shot my sister and her child last night."

She did not need a sermon, spiritual counseling, or a "Thus sayeth the Lord," to sense that God was pouring love into her. I was not remotely aware that God was saying to me, "Signa, that girl has a tragedy in her life. Prophesy to her and tell her I love her." I was only aware that when I saw the pain in her face I knew what she needed. **I couldn't help but tell her!**

In a very real sense this was the prophetic gift in operation – speaking God's words into another person's life. It only came because I knew from experience that God's love covers any circumstance and brings healing. I knew it because I have spent time with Him and am so certain that He loves and heals that I will tell anyone. I simply said to her what God has already said to me.

Occasionally, God may instruct you to give a deliberate personal word to someone. This has happened to me a few times. Being a prophet is not my identity, but God will use me if I am available and willing to speak a prophetic word when He asks me to. Perhaps the person who needs the word from God is not listening to Him, or is involved in sin and needs to be rescued by God, or is about to make a wrong decision about something very important, or needs a confirmation about something God has already spoken to his heart. In His love God often intervenes in our lives when we are in such situations. And He will use those who are listening to Him and are willing to be available for such an intervention.

I confess that in each instance when He told me to speak to someone, I didn't want to do it. Because prophetic words may interrupt a familiar path where a person is traveling, the message is not always welcomed by the recipient with an open heart and gratitude to the prophet. The recipient may even be quite defensive and may lash out against the messenger. I have experienced this and it's not pleasant. However, in each case God used the words I delivered anyway.

Prophetic words are sometimes "get-off-your-rear-end" boosts we need when we have become lethargic. They can be affirmations about something the recipient has already heard from God and either ignored or forgot. They can be warnings to the recipient because God sees a person's life in crisis or turmoil and wants to intervene and rescue. Sometimes the recipient doesn't want to be rescued. Realizing that messengers are often "shot," I often tend to be reluctant to get involved. Maybe you do, too.

It's important to remember, however, that when God tells you to do something, you are not doing it alone. He is with you when you speak. He will also do the follow-up once the word is delivered. He takes responsibility for the consequences. It is not your burden to carry around. Your choice is to put your relationship with Him above any relationship you have with the person who needs His word. This is not always easy, but in **every** circumstance where this has happened to me, I have seen fruit come from the encounter. It was seldom immediate, but over time, God used the words He told me to speak to bring His will to someone's life. Sometimes it was to set someone free, or rescue someone from an impending implosion, or guide someone through a crisis. Years afterwards I have had these recipients tell me something like this, "I was really upset with you when you told me that, but it was the very thing I needed to hear." Or, "I was angry with you for months until God showed me that what you said was exactly what I needed to hear." It truly is better to please God than to please people!

One day God told me to go to a professional young man with a strong word about where his life was heading if he didn't repent of a sin in his life. At the time I had no idea what the sin was. God didn't tell me that. Oh, how I didn't want to do this! I tried to get Conlee to do it for me. He said he would go with me but I had to deliver the message because God gave it to me. He was right.

Before I met with the young man, I found out from another person what the sin was. It was serious. But God had not revealed it to me. I had to be true to the word I received from God. So we made an appointment, and I delivered the message **exactly** as God directed without any accusations or acknowledgement that I knew any specifics. I prayed that it would be delivered and received in love. It hit the mark! God does that. A family was healed.

I have to be very careful that my identity does not depend on whether or not the person accepts the word I bring. They don't have to believe me. I don't have to argue with them. If they don't accept what I say, it is not my responsibility. I deliver. I leave them in God's hands.

But it is vital that I know that it is God who speaks to me, who leads me, and who brings order into someone's life. I cannot be the Lone Ranger, attempting to right all wrongs. I cannot be a person's Savior. I must hear God clearly. I am to obey in love.

> *How is God using you in prophetic ways?*
> *Using Paul's words, decide to eagerly desire*
> *the gift of prophecy from God.*

When you are the recipient: Sometimes a person, without knowing any of your circumstances, will give you a prophetic word from God that is truly like reading your mail. This has happened to me a few times and it definitely got my attention. God spoke to me through the prophetic words of others to point me in directions I probably would have ignored otherwise. Mostly, either the words themselves that came through the prophet or the circumstances that came to pass after the prophet spoke to me were confirmations of ways God was already working in my life. But God had already spoken to me. The inner voice of the Lord to me was simply illuminated and confirmed by what the prophet said.

I have also had the experience of having a man, **who called himself a prophet,** speak into my life with a message that was not from God. What he said sounded good. It even had a ring of true details around it, but the core of the message was from the spirit of the world, not the Spirit of God. John tells us,

> *"Dear friends, do not believe every spirit, but test the spirits to see whether they are from God, because many false prophets have gone out into the world. This is how you can recognize the Spirit of God: Every spirit that acknowledges that Jesus Christ has come in the flesh is*

155

from God, but every spirit that does not acknowledge Jesus is not from God." (I John 4:1-3a)

This happened when Conlee and I went to a public meeting one night at a church at the invitation of a friend. We did not know the man who was introduced to be the speaker that night. We had no idea he was known as a prophet until he told us – for over an hour – lauding himself and his spiritual credentials. I turned to Conlee and whispered, "When is he going to talk about Jesus?"

We heard story after story about how he had spoken prophetically into people's lives and been accurate. He told us so much about himself and so little about Jesus that we were ready to leave at the first opportunity. My spirit already **knew** that this man was **not** a prophet. John's test (see above) was right on: this man was not acknowledging Jesus, but lifting up himself.

Just as he was winding up his self-aggrandizing talk, we were getting our things together to slip out when he pointed to the two of us and asked us to stand up. Well, what do you do in such a situation? Taken off-guard, we stood in the midst of several hundred people, many of whom we knew. And he began to "prophesy."

On and on he went with things that built **us** up, giving us far more importance than anyone should have, holding out promises that were outlandish, declarations of fame, fortune, and the wisdom of Solomon, lifting us up as spiritual super stars. Even as he spoke, it sounded in my ears like the lures Satan lifted up to tempt Jesus in the wilderness. Much to my surprise there were ohhhs and ahhhhs from the crowd as if affirming what he was saying. I was horrified. I even felt slimed, as if I had been to a psychic guided by a spirit of divination. Then, as if that wasn't enough, as soon as he finished speaking his wife handed us a cassette tape of what he had just "prophesied" over us, with information about how we could monetarily support their ministry. We left!

It was not difficult for us to discern that this man was not a Godly prophet. All we had to do was listen to God's Spirit within and not be swayed by his flattering words or the emotions of a crowd around us. The man was revealed to us as a cheap counterfeit of a true prophet. John makes it very clear that the One who is in me is greater than the one who is in the world.

> *"They are from the world and therefore speak from the viewpoint of the world, and the world listens to them. We are from God, and whoever knows God listens to us; but whoever is not from God does not listen to us. This is how we recognize the Spirit of truth and the spirit of falsehood."* (I John 4:5-6)

Although I discerned correctly that this man did not speak the wisdom of God, for many years after this I was extremely leery of **all people** who were known as prophets. This was an immature reaction on my part, not far removed from the way I, as a ten year old child, put the Bible in my bottom drawer when I was afraid I might be deceived. I have since repented of both actions and asked God to reveal to me the true blessing and gift of prophecy – and He has! The Spirit within me bears witness to the Spirit of God.

Years after this event, and after much enlightenment from God, we were in another meeting in a church, at the invitation of a pastor friend, listening to a guest preacher we did not know.

Her message for about an hour was powerful, lifting up Jesus and giving us Biblical principles for overcoming hardships in our lives. It was full of God's love and redemption and filled us with hope and excitement for His plans for us. We had no idea she was known as a prophet. When we thought the service was over, she pointed to the two of us and asked us to stand. *Oh no! I've been here before. Déjà vu! Please don't, Lord!*

She spoke pointedly to both Conlee and me, saying some extraordinary things about us that she could not know, but the message was one of encouragement and direction, not self-aggrandizement and flattery. In an effort to make very clear what she was hearing from God, she even spelled out some of the words. We didn't understand all of the meaning or how it fit together, but we were impressed to write down every word and listen to God. Not many weeks afterwards an unexpected phone call came from an unknown person out of state, who repeated the exact words from the prophet in a proposal for ministry. It was so exact that this caller actually spelled out the same words in the same way!

This story sounds like a "slam-dunk." But it isn't. Although every circumstance lined up and was confirmed and was based on something God had already placed in my heart, the proposal for ministry fell through. Now what were my choices? Discount prophecy once again? Not trust the gift? Give up?

I may be slow, but I learned my lessons from God! I wrote it all out in my Listening Prayer Journal, asking God to clarify all the confusion and get me on His path. His answer to me was not in specific words, but His clear response was to put a fire in my heart for the very thing the proposal was about. He was energizing me into the same arena, but this time it was not dependent on the actions of others but on my collaboration with Him. I am still incredibly excited about this venture although the fruit has not yet been realized.

On another occasion a woman whom God often uses to speak prophetically to people approached me after church. She said that she had "a word for me from God" about one of my family members. I sensed God's presence all over the primary word she had and I was grateful. But then, continuing in the same authoritative voice, she began to give me her interpretation of the word and her instructions for the application. She even said that if I didn't do it exactly the way she described that God's will would be thwarted. It was so apparent that something very beautiful had just turned an ugly corner. She had inserted so much of herself into a truly prophetic word from God that it made the whole thing look tarnished. It is good to remember, as Paul said, *"we know in part, and we prophesy in part."* [34] Instead of my throwing out the words from God along with her human interpretation, I chose to ask God to sort it out and to refine the gift He placed in that woman, realizing that we are all human and will both speak and receive in part.

All of these examples point to the fact that prophecy is never intended to replace an intimate direct conversation that God wants to have with you! Words are to be submitted to Him, refined by Him, directed by Him, sorted out by Him, and ultimately surrendered to Him. This is where a Listening Prayer Journal shines!

Write in your Journal the words you receive either from God directly or from a person God uses to speak into your life.

---

34   1 Corinthians 13:9

Then you will have them intact, to recall, to pray, to seek further confirmation, to prevent distortion, to let Him separate solid truth from fluff, to have a holding place for them until He completes His purposes.

If you have received a word from God through a prophetic person, keep asking God about it if it seems confusing. Write down what He says. Keep listening. When you are disappointed, ask Him again. He is speaking to you. He knows what will get you to the next step better than you can imagine. He has a plan for you and He is orchestrating your personal plan because He loves you. He will show you little by little the revelations of this plan as you listen. It may seem incomplete at times, but it will be revealed in His time. You have access to the Source because you are His sheep and His sheep know His voice, and you **can** hear what He says!

Giving a prophetic word requires time and effort on your part: listening to God, asking Him to confirm His directions, and allowing His timing to prevail.

Receiving a prophetic word requires time as well: listening to God, asking Him to confirm the word, and allowing His timing to prevail.

Have you received words over the years that still linger in your life like unresolved issues?
Have you wondered: Was that God? Was it not?
Did I miss an opportunity?
Was that a false prophecy? Was it true?
Write out the words spoken over you, both recent and from your past, in your Listening Prayer Journal.
Ask God to speak to you about them today.

Remember, God Time is ever-present.
If you know you have received false prophecy in your life
(from sooth-sayers, fortune tellers, Ouija boards,
astrologers, horoscopes, or liars), renounce their word
in the Name of Jesus and ask God to replace them with
His words for you!

CHAPTER 13

ONE GOD WHO SPEAKS IN MANY WAYS

Through Holy Silence and Through Impressions

• *Holy Silence*

In the language of God silence truly can be golden. His silence might be pregnant with anticipation, filled with rich revelation, refreshing comfort, or even deep healing. Yet, often we mistake God's silence for the answer, "No," or for His indifference. Silence is hugely misunderstood, avoided, and even feared. Perhaps we have all become too influenced by television programming where silence (or dead time) is devastating. Even when demonstrating something with one's hands, the TV host is required to keep up a patter of speech at all times. Think about the few times you have experienced silence in a church service. It makes most people feel very uncomfortable, as if the service has suddenly gone out of control. We are accustomed to having music, speaking, or both, the whole time. Sometimes at *Journey* conferences we ask everyone to listen in silence to what God is saying to them. We have learned that unless we "give them permission" to be quiet for a few minutes, many will look around confused and ill at ease.

Conlee and I attended a long weekend retreat a few years after we were born again. It was designed to bring people into the presence of God and present His love in ways that would change hearts. The format was well-organized, well-executed, and meaningful – except for the first night after dinner. We were told that in an effort to tune out the world and to tune into God, we all would observe total silence until the chapel service the next morning.

It wasn't so bad keeping silence until breakfast time. But filling plates from the breakfast buffet, passing coffee carafes, and sitting at tables with around sixty people, most of whom you don't know, and saying **nothing at all** was awkward to say the least. Have you ever listened to fifty-nine other people chew and swallow? In the silence it was magnified tremendously.

In this instance the silence was contrived and not at all effective. Instead of promoting God-consciousness, it just produced an extreme self-consciousness.

Taking a "moment of silence" at public events has long been recognized as a way to honor or memorialize people we care about. Some people pray, some think about the honored ones, and some just wait it out. I've noticed the public "moments" we see on TV get shorter and shorter in length.

> *How often do you experience silence with God in the privacy of your home?*
> *Is it as awkward at home as it is in public?*
> *Why do you think this is so?*

A few times in my life I have experienced the saturation of God's Glory in absolute silence. I have seen miracles occur when He takes over in seemingly impossible situations.

Once in Memphis, at a large gathering of Episcopal priests, all of whom were wearing clerical collars as an identity of their calling and authority, God interrupted the carefully planned agenda with holy silence. Undone, because of the profound holy presence that descended upon us, one by one the priests removed their collars, came out into the aisles, and fell prostrate on the floor in humble submission to God. No one needed to explain what was happening. God just did it!

Conlee and I traveled with Leanne Payne, serving on her team for *Pastoral Care Ministries*, during the many years she led conferences. We went to various places in the world and encountered many unusual customs and traditions among different cultures. We saw miracles everywhere we ministered. We experienced God's healing power in the most difficult situations. However, on our first trip to Belgium we encountered something that seemed to be irreconcilable.

We arrived a few days before the conference began and stayed in one of the beautiful little villages near the conference center. At the time I knew very little about the history of Belgium but knew that French, Flemish, and German were spoken in different areas of the country. I was excited to practice my French with French-speaking Belgians in our area. In and out of shops we went and I greeted the shop keepers with a friendly, "Bonjour!" To my astonishment, while many were extremely friendly and helpful, encouraging me in the language, in some places the clerks turned away from me and refused to communicate or to serve us.

A little bit of questioning revealed that the Flemish (related to Dutch and Protestantism) and the French (primarily Catholic) both inhabit Belgium. In one small country the inhabitants harbor major cultural and spiritual differences. As a result they do not trust one another, do not cooperate with one another and do not like to communicate with one another. This has been prevalent for hundreds of years. I was experiencing a deliberate shunning by Flemish shop owners when I greeted them in French.

There were over 800 people at the *PCM* conference. They were from many countries and included a good mix of Flemish and French speaking participants, many protestant pastors and many Catholic priests, monks, nuns and lay leaders. On the first day of the conference, without consulting the conference leadership, a Catholic clergyman announced that mass would be held early each morning for Catholics. A Protestant pastor immediately countered that there would be an early morning prayer meeting for all Protestants. Already, the climate of the fractured culture was infiltrating a healing conference.

A major concern for Leanne and the team was what to do about the Holy Communion service that was always celebrated at the end of any *PCM* conference. Traditionally, it was a time of great celebration for all God had done during the week, and also an opportunity for God to seal His work and speak to the hearts of His people. In a way, it was what we led up to in all we did during the week of teaching and ministry.

When the Catholic clergy heard that we would have a Holy Communion service at the last session on Sunday morning, a bishop's representative announced that Catholics were not to receive the bread and wine at Communion, and in fact were encouraged not to attend at all. Distressed by the turmoil this was provoking, Leanne's team (both her core *PCM* team and the local Belgian team) met on Saturday afternoon to discuss and pray about the situation. Some of the team members suggested that the Catholics and Protestants separate and have their own services. But when we prayed, that didn't seem right to anyone. Some suggested that we not have the Communion service at all. Again, submitting this to God, it did not seem right to cancel it. Even the core team and the local team were at odds about what to do.

Still not sure about how it would be received, the decision was made to go ahead with the Communion service on Sunday morning. When this was announced, discussions among the participants were animated. There was deep animosity on both sides when we came together on Saturday night for a teaching and ministry session. And this was at a healing conference! We were supposed to gather the next morning at the Lord's table in love, with forgiveness in our hearts! It seemed impossible.

As we began to worship on Saturday night before the teaching began, our worship leaders strayed from the planned segment with words on the overheads and led the large group to sing *a capella* the universal worship chorus *Alleluia*. First the worship leaders on the stage fell on their knees. Then from the front to the back each participant either knelt or fell prostrate. Then the singing ceased and for a full 15 minutes there was no movement or sound at all. That is a long time in a crowd. No one shifted, sniffed, coughed, or squirmed. To a person, each one felt the heavy weight of God's Glory fall in a cloud of healing presence.

This was totally un-orchestrated by anyone but God. Within a few minutes His love covered generations of prejudice, animosity and distrust. I don't know how long it lasted after that conference, but I observed Catholics and Protestants embracing one another, blessing one another, and praying for one another. When the Holy Communion service was held the next morning everyone came. Some chose not to receive the elements of bread and wine, but it was not the bread and wine that brought reconciliation; it was the real presence of the Body and Blood of Jesus Himself. It was a miracle!

• *Impressions*

Learning to recognize the fleeting, so-quickly-there-and-then-gone impressions from God takes time, testing and trust. His "voice" does not always come to us in a booming masculine tone, or even in a clear picture. He can speak so subtly that we can miss Him if we are not willing to accept His word however He wishes to send it.

It is impossible to tell someone else how to recognize that divine word for themselves. The ways He communicates to me will not be the same for you. However, when I pray for a spiritual sensitivity to Him I am always surprised at how He answers me, often in unexpected moments.

There is a man I know whom almost everyone else loves, respects and honors. However, I have such difficulty with this man to the extent that I have trouble looking at him or listening to him, and I find myself trying to avoid him. Have you ever had such a difficult person in your life? One whom everyone else seems to find perfect? It was becoming extremely frustrating, and was bordering on extreme critical thoughts about him, even though I kept my mouth shut to everyone. I felt guilty about my feelings and couldn't seem to dislodge them. I confessed them to God over and over without any release.

One day in church during worship, while I was totally focusing on God, a sudden, unexpected POW! of revelation came into my being. It was almost like being punched in the stomach, but it was gone as quickly as it came. God told me in the briefest second what was going on in that man's life and why I was repulsed. I had known it in my spirit, but had no conscious knowledge of it until God imparted it to me. With that briefest impression of truth, my criticism turned into heartfelt prayer for him and his family. I even wake in the night praying for him.

Another time, while praying for a woman who was all over the place with her emotions, not able to identify her difficulties, not able to receive from God, and yet desperate for help, I received the slightest impression you can imagine of a dead dog, of all things. Reluctant to mention such an odd thing, yet frustrated at the futility of the prayer session, I asked her, "Does a dead dog mean anything to you?"

She looked startled at first, and then burst into tears. "My parents always told me they only had me because my brother's dog died. They wanted him to have someone to play with." In an instant, God pin-pointed the source of her sense of never belonging, not feeling wanted, and believing she should never have been born. It was a remarkable healing session after that revelation.

Pay attention to the slightest impressions you receive. At first, you may not be confident enough to act on them or speak them forth, but write them in your Listening Prayer Journal and ask God about them. Soon, you will recognize His voice when you receive these words or pictures from Him, however wispy and brief, and you will be astounded at what He will do through you!

HOW ARE YOU DOING WITH YOUR GOD MONTH?
What did God say to you today?
In the Bible? In a dream? In a recent sermon? In a book?
In worship? Through others? In quiet?
Through an impression?
Write it all in your Listening Prayer Journal!
Let each way He speaks be an opportunity for
dialogue with Him!

CHAPTER 14
IMAGINE THAT!

It's common for people to think of the imagination as a place within that is filled with fantasies, untruths, futile wishes and possibly dark crevices where evil resides. We learn this as children when we have bad dreams or nightmares and parents tell us, "That's not real; that's just your imagination!" We learn this when we dare to dream largely and someone deflates our dreams with, "Don't let your imagination run wild!" Or, "Don't start imagining things!" We learn this when we hear twisted interpretations of Genesis 6:5. *"And God saw that the wickedness of man was great in the earth, and that every imagination of the thoughts of his heart was only evil continually."* (KJV) Often all we remember about this biblical account of the days of Noah are: *wickedness / imagination / heart / evil.* We lump them together and label *imagination* as something suspiciously unholy, perhaps even evil. As a cumulative result, the mysterious *imagination* becomes something we think we should avoid if we want to stay pure and holy in God's sight.

What an injustice to a holy quality God put in each of us

who bear His image! First, let's examine the Genesis scripture that gives imagination so much bad press. The Hebrew word used in the King James for imagination is *yetzer* which means "intent, purpose, a form." It is clear to see that God saw the *intent* (or what had been *formed*) in men's hearts in the time of Noah was evil. They had forgotten the God who made them and whom they were made to worship.

The same word *yetzer* is used by David in his prayer to God about the attitude of thanksgiving and generosity he saw in the people: *"O Lord God of Abraham, Isaac, and Israel, our fathers, keep this forever in the imagination of the thoughts of the heart of your people, and direct their heart unto you."* (1 Chronicles 29:18, KJV) If the imagination of the heart was declared "evil" by God, then how can David pray such a prayer? Instead, David is saying to God that an attitude of thankfulness and generosity had been formed in the hearts of His people because they had turned back to Him.

Our imagination therefore, can be used for evil intents or holy intents. What determines the content of the imagination of the heart?[35]

Picture This!

Your imagination is a God-given part of who you are. It's God's plan for you to imagine, and He loves to use your imagination for His holy purposes. As we see Biblically, and as we know experientially, imaginations can, indeed, become corrupt-

---

35   Remember the definition of "the heart." It is the assimilation of the thoughts of the mind (knowledge) and the experiences we have (emotions and feelings).

ed. Some imaginations can be so full of horrible, evil, disgusting, destructive images that one wonders if God would ever be able to bring redemption. The Bible says that when He saw such corruption in the days of Noah, it grieved God and filled Him with pain.[36] At that time in history God cleansed the evil from every inclination of the thoughts of people's hearts by means of a destructive flood. But, in Genesis 8:21 He promised that He would never again cleanse the earth in such a drastic way. However, He does continue to cleanse hearts and imaginations today; He just does it in a much different way than He did in Noah's time. Now He accomplishes this deep work of renewing our polluted imaginations through the cleansing, healing power of His Holy Spirit. In each individual who yields to Him, a flood of cleansing streams washes away the residue of evil that might be buried deep within.

If I could draw you an illustration of what the human imagination looks like, I'd draw a blank screen, waiting to have something projected onto its surface for you to see. Of course the actual imagination is much more mysterious and complex than this, but the simplicity of this concept actually helps define a Biblical truth. The screen is neither good nor bad. It is simply a blank canvas waiting for an image. It has no worth to you at all – **until** images are projected onto it. When images are projected onto the screen, you don't focus on the screen itself; all you see is what appears on it.

The images that appear on the screen of your imagination are projected either by yourself or others, including God. Your imagination can be filled with beauty, holiness and creativity, all reflective of God's Glory and presence. Or, your imagination can be filled with terrifying thoughts and images, pornography,

---

36   Genesis 6:6

fearful circumstances, worst-case scenarios, war, or horror. Your imagination is affected by things you read, look at, hear about, who you listen to, activities you do. Just living in the world corrupts one's imagination daily. Whatever is learned and experienced is projected onto your imagination which is a faculty God gives you to reveal what is in your heart.

In your imagination (your screen) you entertain whatever comes from the source (your heart). Remembering that your heart is a combination of your knowledge and your experiences, it just makes sense that if you fill your mind with evil thoughts and plans and reinforce those thoughts with evil experiences and activities, your heart will be evil. Thus your imagination will be filled with images related to such a heart.

Evil thoughts and plans + Evil experiences = Evil heart

If your heart or physical body has been affected by fearful experiences, abuse, terror, and threats of death or abandonment, your imagination will be filled with such images.

However, if your heart has been enlightened by worship, truth, beauty, things that are pure, good, worthy, and lovely,[37] your imagination will be filled with images related to this source.

Godly thoughts and plans + Holy experiences = Pure heart

Your imagination reflects the intent of (or what is formed in) your heart.

Some of the intents of your heart, whether good or evil, are there **by your own choice**. You pick the channel on television.

---

37   **Philippians 4:8**

You click on the website. You open a book. You decide to engage in certain activities. You enter into a conversation. They all leave impressions that affect how you perceive life.

Other intents of your heart are **involuntary**, again whether or not they are good or evil. What were you exposed to at an early age? Were there things that robbed your innocence, or was there good nurturing, both physically and spiritually? Were you victimized, or were you protected and safeguarded? Did you witness horror against your will, or were you put in environments of holy affirmation and God-consciousness? Were you surrounded by sinful, worldly values and images or sacrificial love and encouragement? You didn't have any control over these things when you were a child, but they can greatly affect your heart today.

Hearing God When You Have a Defiled Heart

Any of these negative circumstances, whether voluntary or involuntary, affect the heart and the imagination in much the same way – they defile. When we come before our holy God with a defiled heart, seeking to know what He is saying, it is difficult to hear accurately without distortion and to receive from Him without fear and distrust.

But when we come to Christ, confessing our sins (both those we have committed and those committed against us) and receiving His Spirit, He takes our sins away, forgives us thoroughly, and cleanses us from all unrighteousness. [38] He then gives

---

38   1 John 1:9

us a new heart, one that is undefiled. [39]

Although He cleanses you and gives you a new heart, why is it then that so many of the old images remain within you to continue to distort truth, to tarnish the image of God, and the image of who you are in Him? This can be very frustrating when you have done everything you know to do.

Very dejectedly, one man told us about how frustrated he was every time he came to church. His story was this:

I led a very ungodly and immoral life for many years. There were several wives and several women outside of marriage and I treated them all badly. I have made good money as a doctor but I've squandered most of it. I drank too much, partied too much, got into pornography, gambled, and spoke coarsely. A few years ago I gave my miserable life to Jesus and He saved me in a glorious way. I know I am forgiven and I am genuinely excited about serving Him. The problem is that when I pray or when I come to the Holy Communion table at church, all these old pornographic images come up. I haven't acted out any of them since I got saved but I can't get rid of them. It's as if I am polluted and am never going to get free from my past. I feel like the devil has more power in my life than God does. I spend all my prayer life just pushing down images and rebuking the devil. Instead of feeling close to God, I feel dirty.

God gave Conlee the wisdom to minister to this man. Here is what he told him:

---

39   Ezekiel 36:26

The activities, the sins, and the debauchery of your past have left a residue on the screen of your heart and your imagination. What if instead of assuming it is the devil tormenting you every time you come close to God, that it is God Himself bringing the residue to your attention, wanting to cleanse every remaining stain of pollution from your soul? Try this the next time it happens: Instead of pushing down the images, allow them to come up. See Jesus with you. Hand Him the junk that surfaces. Symbolically, put a hand to your head and to your heart, pulling them out and placing them in His hands. It might even seem like a movie reel of images, or a collage of impressions. As you give it all to Him, watch to see what He does with all of it. Take your time with it and allow Him to show you if there is more. Give it all to Him. Then, let Him replace it with something of His choosing. Let me know what happens.

It didn't take long to hear what happened. The very next Sunday in church, this man ran toward Conlee, oblivious to all the people around him, shouting, "It worked! It worked!" When they had the opportunity to talk privately, he said that he let the disgusting images and memories rise to the surface and did indeed see Jesus standing before him, with hands outstretched, ready to receive whatever he chose to hand Him. One by one, He took every disgusting thing and either destroyed it or transformed it into something beautiful. He just kept saying, "It's a miracle!"

Yes, it is a Miracle!

Living with Jesus is a life full of miracles. However, allowing Him to cleanse the polluted residue of the past from our imagination is a miracle we often ignore. And yet, one He loves to do.

Images from the past might arise at odd times. The devil does try to use any remaining traces of a life once committed to him to accuse us, to tell us we should turn back, to tell us we are no good, to tell us that Jesus' work in our life is insufficient, basically, to tell us that "a leopard can't change his spots."

But, remember who the devil is: he is a liar, a deceiver, an accuser, and he is already defeated. The good news is that "*He who is in you is greater than he who is in the world!*"[40]

Changing the Leopard's Spots

One might argue, "But you can't change the past. You can't make those terrible things I did – or those terrible things done to me - just not happen. They are reality. Not even Jesus can change history."

One of the most amazing things about Jesus is that He takes reality (even the worst parts) and uses it for His purposes which are always for good. The very worst thing I ever encountered, when submitted in its entirety to Him, can be used for His glory and for my spiritual maturity. I have seen this happen so many times it is hard to choose only a few stories to share briefly with you. There are volumes! Each could be a book.

Ron served in the U.S. Army in Viet Nam. He was commanded to do atrocious things to other human beings day after day for months. As a result of his sense of filthiness over what he had seen and done, he came to Christ when

---

40   1 John 4:4

he returned home. Thinking his salvation experience would take away all the horrific images of war embedded in his soul, he was devastated to realize that they now popped up in his sleep. His wife said that although it had been years since he returned from the war, he had nightmares every night, waking up screaming and in cold sweats. Participating in a group prayer that Conlee and I were leading at a weekend retreat, Ron asked the Lord to show him one symbolic memory out of the many atrocities of wartime and then he gave it to Jesus. Ron had never heard God speak to him before, but in that moment he heard Jesus say, "Confess your own sins and then forgive the U.S. Army." It didn't make much sense to Ron but he did it. He confessed the sin of murder and he simply said, "In Jesus' Name, I forgive the U. S. Army." Then he watched Jesus take the specific memory he gave Him, and with it, cleanse all the other memories with His Blood. Wartime blood became covered with the Blood of Jesus. Many years later his wife reported that he had no more nightmares after that prayer session. Although Ron could still recall incidents of the past, they no longer defined him. Jesus now defines who he is. *Alleluia!*

Ron's experience reminds us that sin is a huge obstacle in all areas of life, whether it's the sin of others against us, our own sin, or sin we witness around us. Sin binds evil and evil images to the soul. I'm not sure Ron realized the importance of what he was doing at the time; he was just obeying what God showed him to do. But when he confessed his own sins against others, and received God's forgiveness for whatever atrocious acts he had committed during the war, he was turning loose of the images of war that had accused and plagued him for decades. When he realized how much he hated his superiors who had ordered him to commit the atrocities, he was willing to forgive them. He intuitively knew that by forgiving he was not saying that what they did or ordered him to do was acceptable. Rather, he was saying, "I will no longer be bound to what they did. That is not my identity. I turn them loose. I will not allow them to continue to hold me captive by their sinful ways." In the act of "forgiving the U.S. Army," he was releasing every vile, frightening image of war to God. What had been bound to his imagination by unforgiveness, was cut loose. The results of this spiritual transaction had long-lasting effects on his physical body as well as his soul. He continues to hear God and no longer has nightmares.

Amy watched her husband of over 40 years die of a massive heart attack in their home. After calling 911 she was helpless to do anything to revive him. She watched in horror as his body was violently shocked by the resuscitator when the paramedics arrived. The image of strangers taking away his lifeless body became embedded in her soul. At the cemetery after the funeral she and I talked for a few moments while standing away from the crowd. Amy, always a very strong, no-nonsense person with a take-charge personality, uncharacteristically spoke to me in a very vulnerable way. She told me that every time she closed her eyes she saw her beloved husband, not as she wanted to remember him, but as he looked in the throes of death. She felt she was being tortured. I very simply told her to let that image arise right there and give it to Jesus who most assuredly was with us. She closed her eyes and did so. I watched the most peaceful look come upon her face as she saw Jesus taking the man she loved so dearly into His arms and blessing him with eternal wholeness. She saw her husband healthy, in the prime of life, completely at home with the Lord. It was a miracle! Amy continued to grieve her loss in a healthy way, but from that moment beside a car at the cemetery she was able to access her fondest memories of her loved one. *Alleluia!*

Amy's experience is not unusual when one experiences the death of a loved one. When my mother died, I would wake in the night, vividly reliving the experience of her death. Not until I chose to see Jesus with my mother in those moments was I able to be released from tormenting images of death.

Leah was abused as a child – over and over and over – in unspeakable ways. Christian symbols were distorted in this abuse. Authoritative figures who represented God to her were the perpetrators. Her whole world became horribly confused and she found a place deep within her soul where she could will herself to hide to avoid facing the reality of her life. Although providing a refuge for herself as a child, this "hiding her real self away" was destroying her present relationships and increasingly destroying her ability to function as a responsible adult. Leah had been in therapy for many years learning to cope with the tragedy of her childhood. In prayer, she hesitatingly, but very bravely, allowed Jesus access to a buried, abusive memory. She was certain that He had abandoned her, because she thought He would never have allowed such things to happen if He had been present. But, as instructed, she invited Him into the memory and **chose to look for Him** rather than her usual focus on the perpetrators and the immensity of her fear. Astonished at what she saw, she cried out in love to Him. He had been standing with her all the while, weeping. She knew in an instant that He completely understood. She intuitively knew that He was experiencing what was happening to her as much as if He were the victim. She turned her face towards Him and was filled with His healing love. In her struggle towards wholeness, Leah now has a Rock of Reality to rest upon. *Alleluia!*

Leah is only one of many men and women who have had something so horrific happen it seems to permanently alter the course of their life. Many of them spend a lifetime either in therapy or medicated, or both. Some are self-destructive in many ways. They cannot adjust to a normal life because of the pressure they constantly feel from the pain of such trauma. Typically, secular therapy helps them cope as Leah's therapy did, but Jesus wants us healed, living an abundant life, not crippled forever and striving to manage our pain. Without minimizing the effects of such sin, I can say without hesitation that the pathway to coming free from the effects of such atrocities is always to forgive. This is a fearful thing to hear when one has been consumed by terror, hatred, and shame since the events happened. One of the major lies the devil tells us is that forgiving someone means you are saying it didn't matter. How far that is from truth! Forgiveness means that someone else carries the burden! As Christians it means we give the sinner(s) over to Jesus. No longer do we have to bear the brunt of what they did to us. We give up all claims to be their judge and jury because only He can fill those roles.

We do not have the power or authority to forgive sin. Only God forgives sin. We are to forgive sinners. Forgiveness is powerful. It changes hearts. It heals relationships. It also paves the way to conversation with God!

Jenny called me in a panic. One of her very young daughters had witnessed something that could easily rob her of her innocence. As a result the child had withdrawn from the family and spent time alone in her room, not wanting to talk to anyone. Jenny didn't know what to do. *Do I try to get her to talk about it? Do I not mention it? Do I take her to a professional? I need help!* I suggested that Jenny first ask her daughter if she would like to do something fun with Jesus. Ask her to picture Him right there with her in the garden of her heart. Let Him show her what is growing in her garden. Then, ask Him to pull up anything in the garden that is not supposed to be there, like things that are scary or confusing or ugly. Then watch what Jesus does with the things He removes. Then see what He puts in her garden to take their places. Her daughter was willing to do this and with her eyes closed, she very easily saw Jesus with His hands held out to her. Jenny watched as her daughter quietly completed the transaction. Her little face told the story without her having to recall any details of the experience. She told her mother that when she gave her bad pictures to Jesus He blew on them and they became beautiful flowers and He gave them back to her. She said, "They are my favorites!" *Alleluia!*

Children have open imaginations that can be used in marvelous ways for God's purposes. While it is a joy to watch a child interact with an imaginary playmate, or play house, or play school with vivid scenarios and conversations, never underestimate the power within a child's imagination for healing. Many children who have been neglected, abandoned or abused are lovingly adopted into families who desire the very best for them. Several of my friends have such children, and although they never second guess their decision to adopt, they are frustrated at times by the inherent difficulties within these children that extravagant parental love and provision don't automatically heal. These children cannot access the memories of their earliest days, yet many persist in confusing feelings of not belonging, rebellion, anger, distrust, etc. Giving them opportunities to see Jesus, as Jenny did with her daughter, allows Him to access areas no one else can reach. His words to their heart, or the pictures He shows them, or the impressions He gives can bring deep healing of old scars. These "let's go meet Jesus" times can bring great joy to both parents and children.

Sometimes there is just a dis-ease within someone without knowing any specifics of what happened to provoke such emotions. Melissa came for prayer with such a dilemma. As so often happens, the dis-ease in her soul was translating into physical disease in her body. She had no idea how to pray. She said that although she had experienced this sense of dis-ease within herself as long as she could remember, she grew up with "perfect parents" who were foreign missionaries, "no family problems," "no traumatic events," and an "uneventful childhood." Something about all this perfection just didn't ring true. So we asked her if she would allow Jesus to bring up a specific **memory of His choosing** from her past that might be symbolic of the origin of her problems. We encouraged her just to focus on Him, not to strive to remember anything in particular, but just let Him take her wherever He chose, and to give voice to whatever He showed her. To our surprise, she burst into tears, crying out, "I **can't** remember that! I'm not supposed to! I can't go there!" The memory Jesus accessed was only one of many severe physical punishments done out of cruel anger by her father. Her mother had instilled in her that she must never tell anyone about how he lost his temper because they had to protect his reputation as a well-loved missionary on the mission field. Her body was storing the memory that her mind refused to recognize. In prayer, she forgave both parents, and was freed from the effects of their sins. Then she was able to use her imagination to see Jesus in the childhood situations, to hear what He said to her, and to receive His healing flowing into her body. *Alleluia!*

Often when we pray with someone who gets "stuck" and can't seem to make any further progress in their healing process, we ask Jesus to bring up that one symbolic memory of His choosing. He always hits the mark! Without doing this, a prayer session can often become a long, complaint session, rehashing old problems, blaming, explaining, talking endlessly, and accomplishing very little. Jesus often goes right to the root of one's problems, without endless analysis, just by using a person's sanctified imagination. It is important to encourage the person not to strive to remember something, but just to let quick, even fleeting, impressions come to the surface and begin to tell about them. Most people who have never done this before tend to discount those initial wispy pictures or memories. They want to receive a catalog of memories and then pick and choose which ones to discuss. They have to be encouraged repeatedly to give Jesus permission to choose the memory, not choose it themselves.

Just this week I heard about a child in an orphanage in Central America who was creating problems in her school. Her behavior was so bad that she was about to be expelled. A Christian woman prayed for her in just the way I described. The memory that came up was of her late mother telling her she could never do anything right. She had internalized that lie. Encouraged to look for Jesus, the child saw Him in her imagination and heard Him tell her that she could do many things right, and He even pointed out what some of those things were. Almost immediately, her whole outlook on life changed. Soon, she became a model student and excelled scholastically. What she heard in her imagination was real! She let Jesus define her instead of the lie from her mother. *Alleluia!*

Something as simple as watching a chick-flick movie in a home with some friends left me with images I did not expect to see, scenes totally inappropriate for Christians to watch. We turned off the movie and turned the conversation to something much more wholesome. However, the images lingered. I felt as though an unhealthy bond had been created between us by viewing such things together. I don't know if they felt the same or not. However, later that night, I was able to give all the images I had seen and words I had heard to Jesus and receive His beautiful light in their place. Until He reminded me of this I hadn't thought about the incident again, even when with the same friends. He cleansed me. *Alleluia!*

Almost every day our imaginations are imprinted with things we do not need to receive. Inappropriate commercials on television and the radio. Scenes of horror on the news. Magazine covers on view in the check-out lines. Conversations overheard in public places. Rude actions by drivers. Gossip among friends. We have no control over many of these pollutants. We can just ignore them with a "that's just life" attitude. But over time such an accumulation of imprints really does affect our ability to hear from God in the most effective ways. To take the time to regularly ask Him to cleanse my imagination produces some of the most surprising revelations. Often He shows me that some of the things I tend to ignore really bother Him. Not only does He cleanse my imaginative faculties but He gives me a greater sensitivity to keeping myself unpolluted in the future.

Your Holy Imagination

I have been told that Albert Einstein saw the formula for $E=MC^2$ (the theory of relativity) in 1905, as he saw light dancing in patterns in his imagination. I don't know if this is exactly how he arrived at his theory but he did write, "Imagination is more important than knowledge."

Here are two quotes from Michelangelo: "In every block of marble I see a statue as plain as though it stood before me, shaped and perfect in attitude and action. I have only to hew away the rough walls that imprison the lovely apparition to reveal it to the other eyes as mine see it." "Every block of stone has a statue inside it and it is the task of the sculptor to discover it." In his imagination he saw David, the Pieta, Moses, angels, and others.

Agnes Sanford, a great pioneer in healing prayer in the modern church, taught people how to pray for healing by asking God to give them a picture of what the needy person would look like whole and then just pray what they saw. What a wonderful way to pray! It uses the sanctified imagination to see what God sees.

The 20th century French writer, Antoine de Saint-Exupery, wrote, "A rock pile ceases to be a rock pile the moment a single man with imagination contemplates it, bearing within him the image of a cathedral."

Even Napoleon said, "Imagination rules the world."

God created all humans to imagine, to see things that are not yet as though they are. This is what He does in all of creation. He saw you before you were formed in your mother's womb.[41] He knew who you would be and all you would go through before you ever existed! This is divine imagination!

You are made in His image. You have imagination that can be used for His purposes. We all, however, need a house cleaning

---

41   Jeremiah 1:5

of our imagination from time to time. God loves to do this for us! Out of your cleansed and sanctified (set aside for His purposes) imagination you will be able to receive words and impressions from Him much easier. You will be able to picture Him in truth rather than through a warped or distorted impression of who He is. You will be able to pray more effectively as you collaborate with what He shows you. You will be set free in many ways.

WHAT DID GOD SAY TO YOU TODAY?
Did you write it in your Journal?
As you sit quietly with Him, ask Him to show you
any tarnished places on your imagination.
Trust Him to lead you and to take away whatever
you sacrifice to Him.
Give yourself time to complete this transaction.
Receive whatever He gives to you with thanksgiving.

CHAPTER 15

QUESTIONING GOD

Many years ago I was asked to organize a day-long, in-house retreat at our church. Based on the title of a very worldly, popular book at the time, I called our retreat day, "Everything You Wanted to Know About God* But Were Afraid to Ask!" [42] This was a rather provocative title for several reasons but it got people's attention and there was a huge turnout. The format was to invite three pastors from very different traditions to answer questions that had to be submitted at least twenty-four hours ahead of the meeting. People from all three churches were invited to attend. We did not allow any questioning or discussion from the floor.

Seated in comfortable chairs on a raised dais before the crowd we had a Pentecostal pastor from an Assemblies of God church, an Episcopal priest, and a Presbyterian pastor. The pas-

---

42   In 1969, there was a flurry of national attention by a book entitled, *Everything You Always Wanted to Know About Sex* But Were Afraid To Ask*, by Dr. David Reuben. When I was asked to organize the retreat day at our church in 1972, there was still a lot of buzz about the book. Thus, it was a provocative title for a church event.

tors alternated picking the submitted questions from a box, answering them, and then inviting comments from the other pastors. It was a lively day and the points of view expressed by the myriad of questions submitted were all over the map, both intellectually and spiritually. The people who attended were remarkably quiet and well-behaved in spite of being challenged at times in their faith and traditions by what was presented. The opinions from the different pastors were very new to many of the people who attended.

Later, as I received feedback from people who attended (this included people from all three churches), I was astonished at one prevalent, general comment that came in several forms: "It was an interesting day but it made me uncomfortable."

Loyalty to Tradition

I have thought back on this decades-old retreat day from time to time. I am not very proud of being the organizer of such an event. It was not a spiritually uplifting day; it made people feel defensive about their personal beliefs, and it did little to glorify Jesus. But, I learned several general traits about church people by their reactions afterwards.

First, there seemed to be a very smug attitude in each person about the correctness of his/her own tradition. It might be called *elitism*. Second, each person felt that by entertaining new ideas about God and how to worship Him from other traditions, they were being disloyal to Him. And third, they just didn't want to know anything about how to worship God other than what they were already accustomed to doing. They certainly were not open to experiencing anything outside their own tradition.

Obviously, this occurred many years ago at the beginning of a major outpouring of Holy Spirit presence on mainline churches through the Charismatic Renewal. As a result of that renewal, today many churches are much more open to change as the Spirit of God moves in powerful ways. But there is still a remnant of these early attitudes in each of us. We get comfortable, perhaps even complacent, in the ways we "do church" or relate to God, and we don't want to hear of other ways, or, God forbid! be asked to try some of them. We, too, can become defensive, consider our own ways superior, and just prefer to "leave well enough alone." This does nothing to glorify Jesus or to come closer into His heart.

What Are We Missing?

When our youngest son, Ben, was a freshman at Auburn University he had a profound experience with God. For two years he had left his moorings and turned to drugs and drug-related activities. But when, in desperation and fear, he turned back to God, crying out to Jesus, everything changed for him in an instant. He **knew** what it was like to be rescued from the grips of evil and death. He was now going for God with everything he had!

Of course we were thrilled! God had answered our prayers. But it wasn't exactly in the way we had imagined. First, Ben found a group of other young believers in a vibrant Baptist church in Auburn. He called us one Saturday, asking if he had our permission to be baptized by immersion in the Baptist tradition the next day. Our first instinct was to say, "Ben, you were baptized as a child. You don't need to be baptized again." In fact, our Episcopal/Anglican tradition believes in only one baptism, not multiple ones. Traditionally, if a person is baptized as a child, he confirms (at a service of Confirmation) the baptismal vows made for him when he later makes a personal decision for Christ.

But, in spite of the tradition of our denomination, God checked us strongly. We had been praying like never before for a miracle in Ben's life, and now that it came, almost without thinking, we wanted to dictate to God how to do it. We repented of our attitude and blessed our son in his decision to be baptized.

After a few months, Ben began to tell us about an amazing move of God in a revival in Pensacola, Florida. He and several of his friends from an Assemblies of God youth program at Auburn were driving every weekend to the Brownsville Assembly of God Church to be empowered by the Spirit of God. They would drive all night, and then, so they could be assured of a seat, stand in a long line outside all day until the doors of the church opened at 6:00 PM. Then they would leave after the revival around 2:00 AM and drive back to Auburn. Repeatedly, he asked if we would join him there. But we were busy doing church things at home and serving God in the ways we were comfortable. Conlee was pastoring a church and we were caught up in ecclesiastical activities. We were happy for Ben and his new Christian friends, and thought, *Ah, youth! If these extremes are necessary for God to bring Ben back to **where we believe he belongs**, then so be it.*

Then, another phone call from Ben: "Mom and Dad, there are pastors coming to this Brownsville Revival every night from all over the world. I think you all should drive the one hour it would take you to get there. You're missing something God wants for you!" We felt the conviction from God through that phone call. We decided to go the next Friday night. Ben said there was a special section for pastors and their families to sit and he would meet us and sit with us. We were excited to see Ben and to meet some of his new friends.

What a crowd! What electricity in the atmosphere! It was really loud, with all sorts of people milling around, all ages, all varieties of dress, all races, and all expectant. It could not have been more different than our quiet, traditional liturgical services. We were ready to sit anonymously in the crowd and observe what was touching Ben and his friends so deeply.

As soon as the worship music began it seemed that nearly every person ran to the front to dance! Such abandon to the Lord I had never seen! It wasn't the kind of worship we were accustomed to but it was so obviously offered to God from the heart of each worshiper, that we were soon caught up in the Spirit of worship that was present. We assumed that the evangelist, Steve Hill, would come to speak at any time. But no one seemed aware of time. They were following the leading of the Spirit of the Lord, not a written order of worship.

After at least an hour of worship, the Brownsville pastor, John Kilpatrick, welcomed all the pastors and their spouses present and asked them to stand. Since we wanted to remain anonymous as much as possible, we hesitated, but Ben, beaming, pulled us to our feet. There were close to a hundred pastors there. Then Pastor Kilpatrick asked each pastor and spouse to come up on the platform. So much for being anonymous, this was being televised! So up we went with the crowd of clergy.

What happened next was about as far from an Anglican tradition as you go. The pastor said that each of these clergy and family members needed to be empowered by the Holy Spirit in their calling. He said he was going to count to three, then someone would blow the shofar,[43] and then everyone would shout as loud as they could, and the obstacles to God's empowerment in their lives would fall away. I could not imagine! But when it happened, a gust of Spiritual force came and took us all off our feet. There we were in a pile on the floor of the platform and the Spirit of God was moving inside me, changing my heart, softening my attitudes, dissolving prejudice and elitism, lifting the restraints of unyielding tradition, and setting me free to experience more of God's exciting Kingdom.

Conlee and I began to drive to Pensacola as often as possible from that time forward. For five years God moved powerfully in that place, bringing hundreds of thousands of people to Christ, and many, like us, back to a place of excitement, empowerment, and renewed passion to minister as God desired.

Next to being born again in 1972, this experience in 1996 brought the biggest change in my heart up to that time. I am eternally grateful to God, to Ben, and to all those in leadership who yielded to the Spirit at the Brownsville Revival. Without being willing to listen, to question, to taste, and to experience things totally new to me, I would have remained closed to many of the incredible blessings God continually pours into my life. Using unusual circumstances, He had to "jump-start" me into that child-like attitude again, one filled with awe, wonder, and the desire for discovery every day.

---

43   Ram's horn used as a call to worship or battle in the Bible

Confusing Maturity for Complacence

Paul writes a good bit about maturing in the Spirit. He says that spiritual maturity is necessary to build up the Body of Christ. It is the way we attain to the whole measure of the fullness of Christ.[44]We should all desire to move past the "milk" we become content with, and prepare ourselves for solid food. In Hebrews we are told that *"solid food is for the mature, who by constant use have trained themselves to distinguish what is good from what is evil."*[45]

It is eye-opening to read what the Hebrews writer identifies as elementary teachings about Christ. He lists these six: *"(1) repentance from sin, (2) faith in God, (3) instructions about baptisms, (4) the laying on of hands, (5) the resurrection of the dead, and (6) eternal judgment. "*[46]All of these elements are vital to our faith, but the Word says we are to **learn them well and then move on** as God directs, having these as foundations for our grounding. Instead, don't most of us in our churches decide at some point to get stuck in the elementals?

When is the last time you were asked in your church, "What did God say to you today?" How is God speaking to you on a regular basis? Is He continually calling you out of sin (elementary) – or is He empowering you to remain pure and lead others into holiness (maturity)? Is He continually telling you to increase your faith (elementary) – or are you using the faith you have to step out in the area of miracles, signs and wonders (maturity)? Is He continually reminding you of the infilling of the Spirit of Jesus you received at your baptism (elementary) – or is the Spirit in you

---

44   Ephesians 4:12-13
45   Hebrews 5:14
46   Hebrews 6:1-2

collaborating with Him to change the world (maturity)? Is He continually reminding you of His resurrection power (elementary) – or are you living in it every day (maturity)? Is He continually reminding you that there is a judgment that will be eternal (elementary) – or are you living your life open before the throne of God (maturity)?

We all have become content with far less than what God has for us. It is no wonder that so many people approach Christianity as an obligation or even as boredom. We have lost the excitement of exploration with God in His Kingdom. When did spiritual maturity begin to mean that you don't dance and leap for joy in His presence? Or that you must not show any physical signs of surrender and delight in worship? Or that you must only whisper in church? Who made these rules? Surely not God! Instead, He encourages His people to praise with abandon, with extravagant worship, with shouts, singing, dancing, demonstrations of love and adoration.

When Michal, David's wife, saw him worshiping God exuberantly, she scornfully criticized him, embarrassed by his lack of dignity.[47] The last word the Bible says about Michal is that she was barren the rest of her life.[48] Besides the fact that she bore no children, there is a spiritual principle here. Our scorn of exuberant worship causes something to die within ourselves. Each time we criticize, we put to death our child-like capacity to be fully present with the Lord, without self-consciousness and without fear of man.

Question Him in your quiet time today. Ask Him what more He has for you. Ask Him to show you open doors. Ask Him

---

47   2 Samuel 6
48   2 Samuel 6:23

to give you that child-like heart to live in awe and wonder at who He is and what He does. *Delight yourself in the Lord and He will give you the desires of your heart.* (Psalm 37:4) Ask Him for the desires of your heart!

What did the Lord say to you today?
Is God speaking to your heart?
Are you inviting Him to change your life and make you whole?
What new potential blessing has He been prompting you to taste spiritually?
What opportunities to be in His presence have you neglected?
Taste and see that the Lord is good. (Psalm 34:8)

CHAPTER 16

YOU HAVE THE WRONG NUMBER

I get so irritated when I'm expecting a call, quickly answer the phone, forgetting to check the caller ID, and then hear the opening line from a telemarketer, "Hello, Mrs. Bodishbaugh (they always stumble on the pronunciation), how are **you** today?" Or even more irritating, sometimes it's a wrong number and the caller argues with me, trying to convince me that he dialed the right number. Sometimes the mistaken caller will even try it again several times as though the connection will magically change. Eventually, unless you're one who just likes to casually connect with people on the phone (and you've already learned that is not who I am), you train yourself to check your caller ID every time and quit answering calls from certain numbers or unidentified callers. They become more than mistakes. They are a nuisance.

The Triumvirate of Nuisance Callers in the spirit realm consists of the world, the flesh, and the devil. These three clamor for our attention all the time, especially the time we set apart to have conversations with God. They attempt to interrupt our lives so regularly that we can easily spend all our time arguing with them, hanging up after listening to their spiels, or even, occasionally, giving in to their "this-is-too-good-to-be-true" offer of a lifetime. Wouldn't it be great to have a caller ID in your spirit so you could instantly recognize that dreaded opening line, "Hello, how are **you** today?" which is purposefully intended to engage you in dialogue.

Well, glory! You do have such a caller ID! It is a gift that was given to you from God when you became a believer and received His Spirit. It's called *the discerning of spirits.*

For many of us this is like one of those gifts you were given for a rite of passage, such as high school graduation. You appreciated the thoughtfulness of the giver, but wondered what in the world you would ever do with it, so you put it in a box in your closet and it's still there, maybe in its original packaging. Let's find that box of unused spiritual mementoes and look closely at this particular one. With all the voices vying for our attention, we need all the help we can get.

The Bible lists several gifts that we are given by the Spirit when we are born again:[49]

Word of wisdom, Word of knowledge, Faith, Healing, Miracles, Prophecy, Discerning of spirits, Speaking in tongues, Interpretation of tongues

We are told that, *"these are all the work of one and the same Spirit, and He gives them to each one, just as He deter-*

---

49   1 Corinthians 12:8-10

mines.[50]

Without that one specific gift on the list, *the discerning of spirits,* we would be open prey to counterfeits of all the other gifts and seduced into accepting something far different than what we ask for or what God intends. When we engage any of the spiritual gifts in our lives, we need the Spirit's leading to determine and validate their authenticity.

An Example

Many of the above gifts work in tandem. One can blend beautifully with two or three others as the Spirit calls them forth. It is always amazing when this happens. It's even more amazing when the Spirit uses **you** in this capacity! The following example was a turning point for me. After this experience, I was determined to pay better attention to the ways God brings together several spiritual gifts in me for ministry.

I was leading a monthly evening healing prayer service in our church for several months. One night at the end of a service, God prompted me to invite everyone who needed a miracle to come forward for prayer at the front of the church. Many came and I invited others to surround them in prayer circles. The Spirit of God was moving powerfully and I was quietly praying from the front for each of the small groups.

One of the men who asked for prayer was suffering with brain cancer. He had been taking chemo, lost his hair, and had become noticeably weaker. A large group of people surrounded him, asking God for the miracle of healing. As I watched them

---

50   1 Corinthians 12:11

praying for him, I had the most unusual impression that resonated throughout my mind and imagination. I vividly "saw" a picture of God's hand take a sword and cut into the right side of the man's chest, moving around from front to back. Then He took a fire hose and blasted the wound with water, cleaning it out. That was it.

This impression felt like more of a distraction from praying than a word from God, but when I tried to ignore it, the more vivid it became. This was definitely a time for God's gift of discernment! *Lord, what am I supposed to do with such a picture? This is pretty grotesque. Is it a picture I have seen somewhere?* [Is it something from the world?] *Am I supposed to share this? If I do, will it interrupt the flow of the Spirit and the healing prayer that is going on?* [Is the devil trying to put a stop to what God is doing?] *What if I call attention to myself instead of to God?* [Is this a fleshly thought, calling attention to me, diverting attention away from God?] *What if it scares this man and he doesn't receive the benefits of the healing prayer?* On and on I wrestled with whether to "pick up the phone or let it ring." All of this happened in only a few moments.

I was not consciously asking God to show me if this impression was from the world, the flesh, or the devil, but I was asking Him the right questions. The implications of my questions are in the brackets above. I wanted a confirmation from God that I was discerning Holy Spirit and not being used by other spirits. I sensed God said, "Trust Me." So, I did.

I went to the man in the center of the group and said, "I believe God has given me a picture that I don't understand and He wants me to share it with you. Perhaps He'll make it clear to you." I then related simply what I saw. It got very quiet. The group surrounding him looked at me like I'd lost my mind. After all, we were praying about brain cancer. But the man began to cry. He said, "Only my surgeon and my wife know that I have a deep scar that goes all the way around my right side from front to back from lung cancer surgery years ago. Through that surgery God healed me. I think He's showing me that tonight because He is healing me again."[51]

With that, the level of faith to pray for a miracle rose immensely in the group and God's presence became so tangible you could feel it. This is a great example of how several of the gifts worked together that night. First, came a *word of knowledge* in the form of a picture, then the *discerning of spirits* confirming that it was from God and it could be trusted, then a *word of wisdom about* what to do with it, then *faith* arising in the prayers, with *healing* and *miracles* on their heels. The overflow of this touched many other people who wanted prayer that night.

WARNING! A huge danger for any of us is to assume that once God has used me in such a way, now every impression I receive is automatically from Him. It just isn't so! Although I desire more than ever to pay attention to the impressions that come, and I am able to discern His voice much easier than I used to, I can never put the gift of the discerning of spirits back on the closet shelf. I need to seek Him at all times!

---

51   This man was not healed of cancer. Several months later he went to be with the Lord. His wife revealed to me recently that on that night, when he was given that picture from God, he received a deep heart healing that he had longed for all his life. He received God's love in ways that were inexpressible. He was changed by that encounter and she was profoundly aware of the difference it made in his last months on earth.

I'm Not Interested! (Click)

The pressures of the world, the flesh, and the devil are so persistent that we can get used to them, and/or we can get tired of dealing with them. Each voice has a distinctive way of getting our attention and engaging us in conversation. Once they are able to do that, we're hooked and they know it. It may not occur to us that, at any time, we can boldly declare, "I'm not interested in what you're touting," and then firmly disconnect.

Before we talk about the Three Evil Amigos (world, flesh, devil) individually, let's look at some of their common characteristics. They operate in a way that is uncannily similar to the strategies of telemarketers. The following text is from a legitimate website promoting their techniques for successful telemarketing. Brackets in italics are mine.

In his heart, the decision-maker *[that's you and me]* KNOWS he is being manipulated by the salesperson *[that's the world, the flesh, and the devil]* whose every utterance is carefully preplanned to enslave the target person *[that's you and me]* into walking the intended route and committing to whatever awaits at the end of it. It's done by forcing him into a continuous set of choices, of which none is desirable but one is by far the least undesirable. That element has many names but its main ingredient is "enforcement of acceptance against one's own willingness." It's a really simple thing which actually makes it so difficult to grasp and adhere to. You must never try to force the decision-maker into accepting anything. This way, we establish that one needs to avoid any attempt of forcing decisions on the prospect during the first contact. If the first contact is successful and the prospect agrees to another contact, then you have gained some leverage. If the contact says, "Thanks, but we're not interested . . ." from that moment on there's no return. Nothing the telemarketer can say will ever cause the decision-maker to reconsider. [52]

The telemarketers admit that their success rate is only two percent. That doesn't sound like much, but that little bit is so lucrative to them that they keep on in their persistence. Let's look at their strategy to see what you can do when you are bombarded by the same techniques used by spiritual callers that are not from God.

➤ You (the decision-maker) can have the best of intentions to ignore their calls but they are adept at enticing, flattering, tempting, consoling, and lying. You may not realize what you are getting involved with initially. Often it takes the fruit of the encounter (disastrous results) to reveal the true source.

➤ Your awareness that you are listening to someone who is only promoting their own best interests and their own agenda may be vague at first, but there is a discerning presence in you. You have to choose to pay attention to it and act on it. However, once they entice you to engage in conversation you won't pay much attention to discernment, reason and the Spirit of God. This is the slippery slope. When you pass the point of saying, "No!" you are hooked.

➤ You are never forced to listen to these calls. The "devil-made-me-do-it" excuse won't fly. You have a will to stand against other forces. Ask God to strengthen your will.

---

52   Excerpted from www.telemarketingtips.info

➤ Compromise is not an option. If you ever concede that your caller has a valid point in some areas you have started down the slippery slope.

➤ A definitive "NO!" puts a stop to it. This declaration includes turning your back, hanging up, walking away, and setting holy boundaries in your life.

Brief Biographies of the Three Evil Amigos

I hope it's clear that the best way to get rid of the pestering influences in life that vie for our attention is just to "hang up." With that in mind, let's look briefly at the primary distractions that daily attempt to lure us away from God. The sources of these voices will be described in very short biographies because it really isn't a good idea (or necessary) to spend lots of time studying counterfeits of the real thing if you know the real thing like your own face in the mirror.

This is the premise used by the United States Government as the standard for detecting counterfeit money. They teach their people to study authentic currency so intentionally and deliberately that they will instantly recognize the slightest deviation from the genuine printed bills. The Secret Service employees have five criteria to master: (1) the portrait on the bills, (2) the seal, (3) the border, (4) the serial numbers, and (5) the paper.

The counterfeit detectors spend so much time with their microscopes, memorizing each small detail of authentic currency, that when a counterfeit bill comes into their hands they recognize it immediately.

If we make it our intention to concentrate on the following

five criteria about knowing God, we'll be well prepared to recognize the counterfeits:

1. the character of God,
2. the Word of God,
3. the presence of God,
4. the worship of God, and
5. the voice of God.

This isn't even work; these are the most enjoyable things we can do! We immerse ourselves in Him, spend time with Him, read, study and digest His Word, worship with other believers, devote intentional time and space to be alone with Him, recognize how He speaks to us, and learn the intimate loving traits of His character. Just by doing this regularly we will be able to quickly identify the major opposing voices of the world, the flesh and the devil.

CHAPTER 17

THE AUTHENTIC VOICE OF THE SHEPHERD

The Voice of Life

First, looking closely at the Real Deal and not the counterfeits, we discover a voice that brings life out of nothing. The voice of God called forth and blessed all of creation, called out followers to change the world when it went awry, revealed the glories of Heaven, gave the Law, instructed leaders, taught people to worship, punished the rebellious, and led His people to the Promise. This is all revealed in the first five books of Moses – the Torah.

Moses told the Israelites that when they entered the Promised Land, in order not to be devoured by the enemies they would encounter, they absolutely had to hear God over all the other voices. It would save their lives. To *choose life* they had to stay close to God and listen to His voice.[53] God warned them, as He

---

53   Deuteronomy 30:19b-20

warns us, that there are always other voices to bombard us daily. Listening to (and obeying) the wrong ones will cost you your life, and will cost the lives of your children.

Jesus gave this same vital message to everyone He encountered. It was just as important for the Israelites in the first century as it was for the early Israelites about to enter The Land. And it is just as vital for you and me today! If we choose to live and not die, we **must** stay close to Him and listen to His voice.

The Good Shepherd

Jesus used the imagery of sheep to make the ancient truth come alive to first century people. As believers, you and I are often referred to as "sheep" in the Bible. Because it was such a clear example for middle-easterners for thousands of years (and still is), throughout the Bible God spoke often about sheep and shepherds. The reason was obvious; sheep were everywhere. They grazed in the fields, they were in sheep-folds near the villages, they were the prime source of meat for feast days, and they were offered as sacrifices to Yahweh – and to other gods. Sheep were the most ordinary part of everyone's life. So, it's no wonder that Jesus, and prophets for hundreds of years before, used the example of sheep to teach, exhort, and prophesy over the people. The connection could be made immediately.

Jesus calls Himself the chief Shepherd who watches over His flock. He is the good Shepherd who lays down His life for His sheep. He separates the sheep; He judges them. He is the doorway of the sheepfold where they are protected. He was sent specifically for the sheep that are lost. He knows His sheep intimately. They know how to recognize His voice above all the other shepherd voices. His sheep follow Him, not other shepherds who call them out.

With all these references – and many more – we might want to give some thought and attention to becoming familiar with the world of sheep and the language of the shepherd.

Here is what Jesus' listeners knew well that we may not know, may overlook, or may forget: *A shepherd takes the responsibility for his flock very, very seriously.* If he is conscientious about his job, he will even give his life, if necessary, by fending off every enemy. He brings all his healing skills to those who are injured or diseased, and does all within his power to see that the flock is well-fed, healthy, nourished, protected from danger, and nurtured. He spends endless hours in solitude with his flock. He knows the personality of each sheep, which ones are wayward, which ones are needy, which ones are leaders. He is present at new births and cares for the helpless. He finds pastures where they can graze with all the food they need. He finds still, calm water where they can drink without fear. He provides shelter for them during storms and builds warm fires when it is cold. He sets up boundaries for them so they will not wander away into danger. He talks to them, sings over them, and becomes their source of survival. Whether the sheep realize it or not, they are utterly dependent on him for their lives. Sheep do not survive very long in the wild or isolated from the flock and the shepherd.

At times the shepherd will bring his flocks to a central sheepfold (or enclosed gathering place) where the sheep will spend the night. Sometimes several flocks from various shepherds will be penned together in a common holding facility until morning light when each shepherd will come to collect his own flock and lead them to the pastures to graze for the day. You would think this would be terribly chaotic and that the sheep would get horribly confused while mixed in with other flocks. After all, sheep are not known for their intelligence.

But the sheep who have spent time with their shepherd, dependent on him, will hear the distinctive call or whistle or song they have heard from him so many times, and they will separate themselves from the masses and follow their own shepherd. The voice they follow is the voice of the one they have grown to know by long hours spent in his presence and by learning they can trust him with their lives. The shepherd's call to his flock is not loud, not harsh, and not threatening. He may be so quiet that it would be easy for others to miss it. But his own sheep have heard his voice so often that it has become their favorite sound. Sometimes the lead sheep hear the call before the others. Their ears perk up and they begin to head toward the shepherd. Then the others notice, listen for themselves, and follow the call. They willingly go where he leads because they trust him with their lives.

Jesus uses this analogy clearly when He encourages His followers (His sheep) to listen to His voice. He tells them that the sheep listen to the shepherd's voice and each shepherd calls his own sheep by name and leads them out. He says that the sheep always know the shepherd's voice and, because they trust him, they follow wherever he leads. They will never follow a strange shepherd because they do not recognize or trust his voice. This is all in John 10:1-5.

To unbelievers He said clearly and emphatically, "*You do not believe because you are not My sheep. My sheep listen to My voice; I know them, and they follow Me. I give them eternal life, and they shall never perish; no one can snatch them out of My hand."* [54]

Wow! When you start thinking like a sheep, you realize the incredible relationship that Jesus has with us! And the eternal benefits of our relationship! It makes me want to do whatever it takes to learn to recognize His voice more clearly, and to follow Him. What about you?

---

54   John 10:26-28

CHAPTER 18
THE COUNTERFEITS

The World

Now, we'll look briefly at some of the slick imitations of a Shepherd King and His Kingdom. We'll begin with the world, because you can't very well ignore this one. We live smack dab in the middle of it. Bombarded all the time by the world's values, voices, and temptations, we have to be absolutely familiar with the Kingdom of God to be able to see how the world pales by comparison. Without an implanted knowledge of God's Kingdom and the King, the world can look very appealing, visually and physically.

There are two primary characteristics of those who find their comfort and identity in the world: *pride* and *coveteousness*.

Pride says, "I can do it by myself. I am #One. I am master of my own ship. I don't have to be dependent on anyone else, even God.'"

Coveteousness says, "If I only had a little bit more of

what the world offers, of everything my physical senses find appealing, then I would be happy, complete and satisfied."

Both are lies.

Once, while teaching a series of classes on "How to Hear God's Voice in a Loud and Noisy World," I gave an assignment to find the differences between the world's values and God's values on the following topics:

Your money	Your security	Your free time
Your life goals	Your friends	Your children
Your sexuality	Your death	

I asked the class to find scriptures about what the Word of God says about each topic, and also list what the world is currently saying about each one. This was a challenging homework assignment and sharing the results produced an animated discussion in the following week's class. A twist we took, after everyone had shared, was to relate how the world's values about each topic had changed **just in our lifetimes.** It was enlightening for each of us to realize that we could prove the shallowness of the values of the world by our own testimonies. The very worldly values we are asked to trust in, depend upon, and even stake our lives on are so short-lived in just one generation. But the Word of God endures forever!

With God's values in mind about the things of the world, we are called to make important decisions several times a day.

- Am I going along with the status quo?
- Am I going to choose God's way?
- Which one will bring me more instant, temporary happiness?
- Is that what I want?

- Which one will bring me closer to God?
- What is more important to me?

Often when we make decisions to turn away from the values of the world and to embrace God's values, we will alienate family, friends and business associates. Then, more questions arise.

- Will I lose my credibility to witness to them?
- Will I lose my job?
- Will I lose my reputation?
- What is more important to me?

Don't be afraid to ask the questions! It is important to have conversations with God about each one.

Several years ago at a conference Conlee and I led, we invited a long-time friend to share a bit of his story with the group. Immediately, he had their undivided attention when he began, "I was born and groomed to be a prince of this world." He related some of the details of his life that most of us only read about. His very wealthy family had prepared him as the first born son to take over a large international business. He received a fine education, married a lovely wife, owned several impressively beautiful homes, had handsome sons, a large bank account, a corporate jet, and an inheritance for worldly success just waiting. Because we knew him well, we knew that these facts of his life were not at all exaggerated.

Then he paused, sighed loudly, and told the group, "I just recently informed my father that I will not be accepting the position in the family business he has groomed me for. I am choosing a life devoted to Christ." The result was that the father who had lavished worldly goods on his son, now cursed him, threatened to disown him, and told him he was an embarrassment to the family.

The hurt was obvious in his face and in his quavering voice. But then, he said he would like to share in more detail what he was giving up by choosing Jesus over the world and what it offered. Everyone was expecting to hear about large bank accounts, trips, cars, vacations, and worldly pleasures. Instead, he said, "I am giving up adultery, deceit, alcoholism, deception, greed, coveteousness, pride, arrogance, and ruthlessness." His list went on and on.

As his confession continued, you could see more and more peace come upon his countenance. He was taking on the image of Christ, not the image of the world, merely by his declaration. He then asked the group to pray for his father, and for him. Conlee and I continue to enjoy a relationship with this man and his wife, many years after that declaration. He has lived into his calling by God and his decision to find his identity in Jesus and not in the world.

The world's enticement to us can be summed up in this lie: "That which is created will give you ultimate happiness and eternal life." When we begin to believe that creation, rather than the Creator, will fulfill us, we have started down that slippery slope to death. Think of all the ways we fall for this deception. It doesn't have to be nearly as grand as our friend's worldly temptations. We once had a beloved pastor who grew up believing that he would be happy for the rest of his life if he could just live in a brick house. This was the ultimate worldly possession he could imagine because of his very meager upbringing. He had to deliberately resist the temptation to covet a brick house to live in.

On the other end of this spectrum is the well-known worldly billionaire, Donald Trump, who was once asked publicly, "How much money will it take to make you happy?" His response was very revealing. "Just a little bit more."

Most of us fall somewhere in between these two extremes when we think "stuff" will bring us happiness.

But it doesn't have to be physical possessions or money we covet. It can be fame and prestige, pleasure, a certain occupation, education, beauty. . . Whatever is just out of our reach is the temptation of the world. This was the dilemma of Adam and Eve in the Garden. God provided everything they needed and more. They were surrounded by untouched beauty and the awesome presence of the Creator. Yet, the one thing they could not have blinded their eyes to everything else they could already enjoy.

The sensate appeal from the world is as strong as the pull of gravity on our bodies. We can't just ignore what is there. It surrounds us and we live in its midst. But just as Jesus physically overcame gravity when He ascended to the Father, so, in Him, we can overcome the pull of the world on our souls. We can only successfully say, "No!" and hang up on the voice of the world when our hearts are committed to Jesus. He empowers us to renounce the lure of the world and to fully enjoy the benefits of loving Him – giving us what He calls *abundant life.*

CHAPTER 19

THE COUNTERFEITS

The Flesh

This counterfeit can be somewhat confusing because we are told in Scripture to "crucify the flesh,"[55] yet we are also admonished to love our own bodies in a healthy way. We have to do a little digging here to get to the truth and not call the flesh that God blesses something evil.

Biblically, the word "flesh" is used to describe the physical body, apart from one's spirit. Jesus was the spiritual Word, yet made flesh; He had a physical body. But more than that, Jesus personified what Ezekiel prophesied: *"I will give you a new heart and put a new spirit in you; I will remove from you your heart of stone and give you a heart of flesh."* [56] The heart of flesh (as opposed to the heart of stone) that God wants us all to have comes from being able to hear God's voice and obey Him. It is a yielded

---

55   Galatians 5:24
56   Ezekiel 36:26

and worshipful posture towards the Creator.

However, the Bible, apart from describing "flesh" as the humanity of Jesus and the heart God desires to give us, also defines "flesh" as the un-renewed part of each person. If we "live by the flesh" it means we live out of our unhealed neediness that is consumed with a hunger to be comforted. Those who "live by the flesh" attempt to find such comfort by their own means. When we "live by the Spirit," we find our comfort through the Creator.

The voice of the flesh, often to our surprise, usually comes out of our own hearts and our own mouths. It has a whiny, demanding tone, full of self-pity, and a sense of entitlement. *But I deserve it! You don't understand how I feel! No one's pain is quite like mine!*

The flesh loves to be the guest of honor at pity-parties. It loves to talk about itself and seldom listens to reason. It can magnify small things greatly out of proportion, gets its feelings hurt easily, and is hard to satisfy. It demands special attention and rewards. It also can become so focused on its own needs, that excessive self-love turns to destructive self-hatred.

These attributes most often originate from very legitimate needs. However, there is a huge gulf between the desperate voice of the person who submits his needs to God and is anticipating healing, and the needy, complaining, narcissistic voice of the flesh who demands immediate special attention and reward.

An effective litmus test to determine if the voice of the flesh is dominant in your life is to identify the primary sentiments you live with daily. Here are some options:

I'm deprived   I'm entitled   I'm so needy
I'm more special than you are   I deserve it

I'm impatient – I want it NOW   I'm misunderstood
I'm unappreciated   I'm self-conscious
I hate myself   *You may fill in some blanks*

These are common expressions of the flesh. They can be so loud and persistent that they drown out everything else. If some on this list are prominent in your life, ask the Lord, "Why is this voice so loud? Where did it come from?" Listen to what He tells you and listen to who He says you are. Let Him show you how to be healed in your broken, wounded places and put that fleshly sentiment to death.

Through Paul, we know **what** we should do: *"If I am Christ's I have crucified my flesh with its desires and lusts. If I live in the Spirit, then let me also walk in the Spirit, not according to my flesh."* [57]

We need God to show us **how** to do it. How do we kill the flesh? A divine conversation with Him is vital here.

It's important to remember that God blesses the flesh that is in right relationship with Him. He wants you to submit your needs, your pain, even your physical body to Him, so that your flesh (or body) becomes a temple for His Spirit, and you can honor Him with your body and your transformed wounds. This is a huge transaction! It isn't something we decide to do one day and see all the results the next. It takes deliberate intention and time for the healing to occur once the process begins.

If I have surgery, it takes time for my body to recover even though the healing process begins immediately. When I begin to cut away many of my old attitudes and wounds it can feel like major surgery. Submitting my old hurts to Jesus happens little

---

57   Galatians 5:24-25, personalized

by little as I become aware of them. My sins are forgiven at salvation, but I need God's help and some time to let a lifetime of responses be transformed.

I especially need God's help to "crucify my flesh," as Paul describes it. This process can truly seem like I am putting a part of myself to death when I give up (renounce) some things that have provided comfort to me in the past. First of all, I need His help to identify what my inordinate needs of the flesh are. I can very seldom be objective about this aspect of the process. This is one more reason why a conversation with God is so vital! *Lord, what do You want me to deal with today? An attitude? An activity? A misunderstanding?* This is the time for meaningful dialogue with Jesus to let Him set the agenda.

Sometimes it may be helpful to have a listening prayer partner who can help me connect with God. This takes a person who is objective, not overly sentimental, honest with me, and who will point me away from my pain so that I can hear what God is saying to me, not the screaming voice of my flesh.

There are other times that the deepest healing occurs in me when, in desperation, I get away from everyone else and have a retreat time with the Lord.

When the presenting problem is identified by the Lord, it's very important that I declare my intentions. I need to *vocally renounce* the things of my flesh that are not submitted to God. But I can renounce all day long, and until I get to the root of the need that empowered the flesh, it will have no lasting effects. I have heard many well-intentioned pastors and counselors say, "Just renounce that feeling / attitude / sin / unholy desire / activity, etc." They are partially right. The things that draw us away from God must be confessed and renounced. However, the staying power of the renunciation comes when we deal with the source. Example: *Why is there water leaking from my ceiling?* I can clean it up and repair the ceiling until it looks perfectly new, but until I know where the leak originates, it will only do it again next time it rains. The question that must follow is: *What is the source of the leak?* I may only be aware of the "water stain on my ceiling," but the Lord will take me to the hidden source, which is not hidden to Him at all.

God not only sees me objectively, seeing all my stains, He views me through the lens of His infinite love. He never looks at me through the lens of my pain, rejection, failures, losses, or pride. However, until I am healed that is the only way I can see myself. Everything is distorted when I rely on introspection. But when I examine myself in a Biblical way by looking upward and outward to Him, He shows me who I really am and who I am meant to be. Plus, He shows me how I can live into the identity He has for me. He never ignores the "stains on my ceiling." He just doesn't whitewash them. He shows me how to get to the "source of the stain," get it fixed, and get on with life. This can be really hard work, it may involve tearing out some things I spent a lot of years putting in place, and it may be painful. But once the job is completed, I can truly live in a freedom I once only imagined.

Joel had struggled with homosexual thoughts as long as he could remember. He grew up feeling very different from all his friends, and to the best of his ability he hid his inner desires. He was gifted in his work, was married, and had children. But the old feelings remained no matter what he did or how he succeeded in his career. At one point in his life, after much frustration, he decided to give in to his feelings and act on them. It was not at all the experience he had always imagined because the man involved with him was not the idealized person Joel wanted him to be. The experience left him feeling like more of a misfit and a hypocrite than ever before. He was desperate to live without feeling guilt-ridden and frustrated.

Conlee met with Joel one day for coffee and heard his story. Joel was born again and knew **what** he should do according to the Word of God, but he didn't have the strength or even the desire to do it. He confided to Conlee that he had come to the decision that he should quit feeling guilty for the rest of his life, that he was going to let his deep feelings finally reign, and was going to just live the lifestyle he had always fantasized about. He believed that this was the only thing that could make him truly happy.

Conlee listened to Joel's declaration and asked God for wisdom. He then said something very simple, yet very profound. "Joel, you have just chosen death."

In anger, Joel confronted Conlee with, "You just put a curse on me! You can't do that!"

"No," Conlee said, "you have put a curse on yourself. Do what God tells you to do and live."

This got Joel's attention. He took Conlee's words seriously. He asked God what to do. The first thing he sensed God leading him to do was to go somewhere alone, away from all distractions, for a personal retreat. Joel told his family he was taking an indefinite amount of time to get away and he went to a friend's cabin in the woods, an isolated place, far from home. At first he thought he would go crazy. He read, he walked, he cried, he hurt. It took him several days to relax enough to hear God's voice but he was determined he would stay there until he heard God, and when he heard, he would obey.

Surprisingly, God did not start talking to Joel about his *stains*, his behavior and his rebellion. He began by showing Joel the source of his *leak*. The root cause for him was the awareness that he had always been an embarrassment to his father when he was growing up. Joel did not have the personality, the gifts, or the demeanor that his macho father had expected from his only son. As a result, he ridiculed, cajoled, and mocked his son, hoping to shape Joel into his own image of a manly man. But, his actions back-fired. Joel, instead of imitating his father, fantasized about other men affirming him. The kind of affirmation he desired soon turned into sexual affirmation because no other physical image carries the sense of "oneness and attachment" as sexual imagery does. Joel took this imagery upon himself as his identity. It was not God's identity for him, but a decisive, desperate reaction to his father's lack of approval. It developed a life of its own.

For days in the woods, seeing no one, Joel spent time alone with God, letting Him set the agenda. During this time he not only recognized the source of his feelings, he confessed his sins, received God's forgiveness, chose to forgive his father, divorced himself from his father's misplaced expectations, and truly desired to be set free. Many times he declared aloud, "I renounce these desires in the Name of Jesus." Sometimes he even **shouted** them aloud since no one could hear. But there was still something that did not turn loose inside. He knew the old desires were still buried there, just waiting to emerge once more.

He had done all he knew to do, but Joel waited with God, desperately crying out for help, until finally one day he heard the still small voice. It was certainly not what he expected to hear. He didn't even want to hear it. *Kill it! Stick a knife in its heart and kill it!*

Joel's identity had become so entwined with his secret fantasy life of being comforted by a man, both sexually and non-sexually, that the thought of putting it to death was just like contemplating suicide. He couldn't imagine living without the soothing and exciting desires that kept him from feeling empty inside.[58]

Joel, in spite of his reluctance to give up his illusive identity, really loved the Lord. He had been in solitude with Him for over a week, listening to His voice and reestablishing a trust relationship with Him, and he was desperate. When we get desperate enough, we can become very dramatic. Sometimes that is what it takes to obey God. Joel pictured the false image of the man he had become like a ventriloquist's dummy. He even gave him a name, different than his true name. He pictured the kitchen table as an altar on which he took off his false self and laid it down. He took a knife from a kitchen drawer and plunged it repeatedly into the air over the table, picturing himself slashing the dummy until nothing remained. He "stabbed the heart" of the false identity that he thought he could not live without. He *crucified the flesh*. It died then and there, and Joel came home a new man, ready to let God build him up in the right ways. He learned to hear the Father's voice and, from the Father, he received much more affirmation than his broken, earthly father could ever give. He became a man because His Father told him who he is!

This happened many years ago and it lasted. He has become the husband, father, grandfather, and gifted Christian that God always intended.

---

58   I have heard many other people say the same thing when confronted with giving up sinful activities like pornography, adultery, gambling, alcohol, etc. This is typical of addictive behavior to comfort oneself, whether the addiction is to a substance or an activity.

The lethal combination of listening to the voice of the flesh and yielding to its insistent demands is a death sentence. Listening to the voice of God and obeying Him brings life – in abundance.

God wants **you** to have abundant life. He will help you crucify the un-renewed parts of your flesh, while embracing your humanity to His glory. He wants to renew your mind, heal your emotions, be in the center of your disappointments and desperate circumstances, and redeem your flesh. This is transformation!

CHAPTER 20
THE COUNTERFEITS

The Devil

The devil is the one voice of this evil triumvirate that seems to get the most attention from Christians. I don't know why. The more we talk about him, the more he gets puffed up, even if we say something negative about him. I heard a public figure say one time, "Bad publicity is better than no publicity at all." That seems to be the devil's motto. He doesn't care if we bad-mouth him, tell him to go you-know-where, and talk about what a nuisance he is. He just wants us to keep him in the forefront.

Of course, it's foolish to act as though he doesn't exist, but we surely shouldn't be looking for him behind every problem either. And most certainly, we shouldn't ever, ever get into argumentative dialogues with him. Just like when we do this with the telemarketer, that is when we hit the slippery slope with the devil.

Everyone would agree that renouncing the devil is a good thing, that listening to his lying voice will cause us a lot of trouble, and that he never has our best interests as his priority. But it's the subtleties of his antics in our life that trip us up. If he appeared to us in a slick red jumpsuit with a long tail, horns on his head and a pitchfork in hand, how easy it would be to recognize him and tell him where to go! But, like Mr. Grinch, he's not only a mean one, he's a clever one, too.

We can get ourselves in a whole mess of trouble, blaming other people, reacting in appalling ways, yet not realizing until it is way too late that it was the enemy messing with us all along. This is why, without studying his habits in too much detail, we need to be able to recognize the ways he speaks to us, so that as Barney Fife always said, we can "nip it in the bud."

I once met a Bible study teacher who believed it was her moral obligation as a Christian to devote herself to studying Satan and darkness so that she and those she influenced would not be deceived by him. She spent years immersing herself in the study of all sorts of dark religions and practices, thinking she would be more knowledgeable about the devil's tactics. Although she adamantly spoke out against darkness and evil, at the same time she was taking into her soul the knowledge and images of what she studied. Leading a large Bible study in her church, she then shared what she learned with many women, unwittingly pulling them down with her into a web of confusion and frenetic super-spirituality. There was little genuine holy worship of God when they met.

I was an invited guest to speak to their group at a large evening meeting. Coming from another state, and knowing none of the women previously, I could be objective when they could not. We began our day at a luncheon and prayer meeting with the leadership council of the group. Immediately, I could see (and feel) the results of their studies. It took me a while to find out **how** they had taken darkness into their midst, but I was aware of it from the first minutes we were together. Some of the outward signs I observed were: *very fleshly, overly sentimental, artificial ways of relating to one another; loud, screaming, demanding prayers; constant warnings to Satan to "leave us alone, you have no place here, we come against you, etc."* In their prayers, they spoke more to Satan than to the Lord.

Besides their behavior, there was *a lot of show and spiritual rhetoric, but little evidence of a warm, loving relationship with a personal God; little reverence toward the Holy; and a large degree of superstition.* They had developed a formula for prayer that had to be done in a certain way or they believed it to be ineffective.

Later that afternoon I had a chance to speak personally with the leader and learned the basis of this aberrant behavior. Her heart had become so heavy with the burden of the knowledge of evil that she was extremely grateful for the exhortation to renounce evil and invite the Light of Christ to invade her life. She thoroughly repented of her actions and admitted that night to the whole group what she had done. What a courageous act! She put God's truth above her own established reputation, and many women and their families were set free.

So, you might ask, how then do I learn what I need to know about Satan's wicked ways and yet not get sucked in by his wiles? I think there are just two primary things to do: (1) keep all information about the devil Biblically oriented, and (2) pray to God a lot! Here's what I am praying even as I write about darkness:

Holy God, You are Light and Purity. I want to be sur-

rounded by You alone, where there is no darkness at all. I want to be able to choose You in every situation, without compromise. Please open my mind to receive valuable scriptural knowledge, yet be my protector and my defender from anything evil. In the Name of Jesus, I call upon Your wisdom and Your presence to protect me and to reveal to me any ways in which Your truth has been distorted. I will seek Your face and choose to listen to Your voice.

Here's what God taught me about the devil as I **studied His Word.** The Hebrew word *satan* is both a noun and a verb. It literally means, as a noun: "an accuser, a slanderer, or an adversary," As a verb it means: "to accuse, to slander, or to be an adversary." Being a *satan* is Biblically applied in Hebrew to human beings as well as to fallen angelic creatures. It can be used to describe a person who is an adversary, an enemy, or a liar. This was a new concept to me, but when I realized that although we don't call another person, "satan," we do refer to a really bad person as "you devil." So, this makes sense.

In the Old Testament when a fallen celestial being is described as "Satan," there is always a definite article preceding the Hebrew noun (*ha satan* or *the satan*). For instance, the court room scene in Zechariah 3 describes *the satan* standing beside Joshua, the high priest, accusing him before the Lord. It's a wonderful scene because we mostly see the mercy of God as He forgives Joshua and cleanses him from all traces of sin. Although *ha satan* surely thought his performance was the starring role, God upstaged him very easily. All of Satan's bravado and accusations are overshadowed by the main character in the scene, the Lord! Satan is quickly ignored, forgotten, and written out of the drama.

This is the way it should be!

Let's look at each of the three definitions the Hebrew gives to *satan*: accuser, slanderer, and adversary:

- ### *Accuser*

    "To accuse" means to find fault with someone, to blame, or to bring charges against them. When the devil accuses you, it may be about something valid or invalid, but his accusations never allow for repentance. He accuses you to tear you down, diminish you, and make you focus on everything negative with no hope of being set free. If he can get you to accept his accusations and let them become your identity, you feel as though you are marked forever with a sense of unworthiness. It's as though you allow him to tattoo you with his words, imprinting you with his false definitions of your identity. There seems to be no escape.

    This is as far from God's way as east is from west. Satan's goal is to destroy you. But God points out your faults and sins to you (conviction) so that your guilt will lead you to confession, forgiveness, cleansing and freedom from the burden. With God there is always hope and always a way out. *"Godly sorrow brings repentance that leads to salvation and leaves no regret, but worldly sorrow brings death."* (2 Corinthians 7:10)

    A little litmus test you can use when you feel weighted down by the effects of accusing voices, is to ask yourself, "Am I being encouraged to rise up from where I am so that I can be clean and free from what I've done? Or, am I tempted to submerge myself in shame and self-pity?" Your answer will identify the source of the accusations.

    God gave John the following revelation about the downfall

of the accuser:

> *"Then I heard a loud voice in heaven say: 'Now have come the salvation and the power and the kingdom of God, and the authority of His Christ. For the accuser of our brothers, who accuses them before our God day and night, has been hurled down. They overcame him by the blood of the Lamb and by the word of their testimony; they did not love their lives so much as to shrink from death.' "*(Revelation 12:10-11)

Notice that in this scripture the people of God, who have been accused repeatedly by the devil, successfully overcame his tactics by coming closer to God in every way. They entered into the blood covenant with the Lamb of God so that their sins could be forgiven and their stains washed away. Then, they willingly shared with others about what He had done for them. And, finally, they lost all fear of death being the ultimate threat and the end of everything, but they had a vibrant hope of resurrection life with God throughout eternity.

• *Slanderer*

While accusations thrown out by the devil may have some kernels of truth at their core, slander is always false. It consists of blatant lies about a person and it is specifically intended to damage one's reputation and character. The devil will slander God's people of almost anything that will stick. He slanders at every opportunity, spreading lies to us about ourselves and others. Slander is malicious and deliberate. It intentionally tarnishes the character of a person and distorts truth.

The devil slandered the character of God in the Garden: *God knows that when you eat the fruit you'll be like Him!* He was insinuating to Adam and Eve that God was deceitful, selfishly jealous and narcissistic. *Did God really say that to you?* He was insinuating that God could not be trusted to tell the truth. *You will not surely die.* He inferred that God had ulterior motives and was intimidating His creatures.

Slander is a very serious offense. A slanderer attempts to play God, re-forming someone for his own purposes through the power of his words. And the power of words is strong indeed. When positively applied, words can encourage, boost us upward, give us hope, increase our faith in what we cannot see, motivate us towards doing the right thing, and mature us into the full potential God has for us.

My grandmother, Mamo, constantly applied positive affirming words to my heart when I was a child. *I'm so proud of you! You can make a difference! Go for your heart! You can do it!* Those words she spoke to me so many years ago still ring out in my soul. She was probably only saying them when I attempted to turn a somersault, or learn to knit, or arrange flowers with her, but they accumulated and found a resting place in me. I was able to apply them to many more things as I matured because they had power in my life.

I needed her words because many of the other influences in my life were saying things like, *You can't do that! You are an embarrassment! You are just a silly little girl! You aren't smart enough!* Those words had power over me as well and it was a constant struggle to choose which ones to believe.

When we are slandered and accept the lie, we allow a part of our selves to be put to death. *There must be **some** truth in* *what they said or they wouldn't have said it!* This is a primary tactic of the devil. He wants to put to death the best part of our selves, the part that reaches out to God, the part that chooses His voice and His paths, the part that bears His image.

Jesus confronted slander from the devil working through many of the people He encountered. He demonstrated for us what to do when we are attacked by slander:

> *"Why is My language not clear to you? Because you are unable to hear what I say. You belong to your father, the devil, and you want to carry out your father's desire. He was a murderer from the beginning, not holding to the truth, for there is no truth in him. When he speaks, he speaks his native language, for he is a liar and the father of lies. Yet because I tell the truth, you do not believe Me."*
> (John 8:43-45)

Not for one minute did Jesus allow the devil to distort or diminish His character. He knew who He was because He believed the Father. He knew who the devil was because He knew about his origins, his character, and his eventual demise.

• *Adversary*

An adversary is your enemy on all counts. The devil is your personal adversary who distorts truth, accuses rather than exhorts, confuses rather than clarifies, and has as his ultimate goal the destruction of your soul. He has declared war on you whether you know it or not, and his military tactics are sneaky.

The personality of the devil does not play a central role in the Old Testament although his presence is seen throughout.

Don't you know he hates the Word of God because in it he is reduced to such a defeated, minor role! Throughout history the
devil has attempted to defame, dilute, destroy and invalidate the
Bible. He hates truth! He shows up occasionally in The Book in
such roles as the serpent in the Garden who opposes God's will, as
the threatening sea monsters who seek to destroy God's creation,
or as a fallen creature who seeks the downfall of God's servants
(as in Job). In each case, God is the all powerful One, always victorious, who never, ever has His authority threatened or diminished.

Let's look at just one of these exposés of the devil's character: the serpent in the Garden. After all of Satan's bravado and
thinking he had thoroughly thwarted God's plan, we see that God
immediately had the situation under His control. Just because
the results were not evidenced at once does not mean that God's
will was not immediately set in motion. We can make the same
mistake the devil did. We can think that because we don't see
instant results when we pray, that nothing is happening, and assume that God has checked out.

God's way of dealing with the deplorable situation in the
Garden was not to have a roundtable discussion with Adam, Eve,
and the serpent in an attempt to effect reconciliation. He shows
us that His decision is made without debate or dialogue with those
who oppose His will. He simply, yet emphatically, declared that
there was enmity between the serpent and the humans forever.
He then made it perfectly clear that the offspring of the woman
would overcome the power of evil. There was no discussion; it
was a declared fact, a done deal. God's goodness and the devil's
evil would be at odds for all time, but there was never a question
of their equality or of the outcome. God was, is, and always will

be the Victor!

God's decision didn't mean that there would be no fall-out from the Fall. There were consequences that would affect all mankind just as there are always consequences to sin. The eternal, costly results of the Fall remind every descendent who lives just how serious sin is, yet how very much God loves each sinner and the lengths to which He will go to draw us away from the adversary and into His love.

We may be in a war with the devil, but with God, we are on the winning side. When we follow His lead, we will be led to victory!

Deception, Seduction, and Intimidation

The devil has the capacity to make sin appear very attractive to us but he does not have the power to make us sin. How many people complain that they have lost their will power to stand against temptation, sin, or attacks from the enemy? Is it that one morning they woke up to find they misplaced their will power, or it leaked out of them while they slept? This seems unlikely. It is more likely that by the time you realize your will power has decreased, you have been relinquishing bits of your will to the devil all along. There are three primary ways he encourages you to give your will over to him:

1. Deception
Going back to the Garden, remember how the serpent deceived the woman? He did it deliberately, but stealthily, and in stages. First, he planted doubt about the veracity of God's word,

then he struck with the outright lie, then he went in for the kill. Reading the account is like watching a very clever fencing match, only the woman had no idea how to parry with him, and she did not call on God to protect her. Instead, she engaged in dialogue with him, and eventually, handed her will over to his tactics. She did not "hang up!"

Paul described her actions this way:

> *"But I am afraid that just as Eve was deceived by the serpent's cunning, your minds may somehow be led astray from your sincere and pure devotion to Christ. For if someone comes to you and preaches a Jesus other than the Jesus we preached, or if you receive a different spirit from the one you received, or a different gospel from the one you accepted, you put up with it easily enough."* (2 Corinthians 11:3-4)

Paul strongly urges his listeners to stay close to Jesus and let Him lead them, be aware of other spirits that are different from the Holy Spirit, and thoroughly know and depend on the Gospel of Christ.

2. *Seduction*

Again, let's go back to the Garden for the best example. The woman was enchanted by the appearance of the forbidden fruit. *"When she saw that the fruit of the tree was good for food and pleasing to the eye, and also desirable for gaining wisdom, she took some and ate it."* Her free will, given by God and intended to be in submission to His, was seduced away from her because she put more importance on appearances and feelings than she did God's wisdom and love for her.

Outward beauty, glittering and enticing appearances, and the feelings they stir up within us have a carnal appeal to our senses that can beguile us to throw the good of reason to the wind. Paul said, *"It's no wonder, for Satan himself masquerades as an angel of light."* [59] He described some of the manifestations of the devil's imitation of light as *"the work of Satan displayed in all kinds of counterfeit miracles, signs and wonders, and in every sort of evil that deceives those who are perishing. They perish because they refused to love the truth and so be saved."*[60]

By the time Jesus came as Messiah to earth, the devil possessed such an amazing amount of swaggering confidence that he believed he could even seduce the Son of God. The devil had thousands of years' practice (and success) of seducing and tempting God's people to relinquish their will to him. He even convinced many of them that they were like God, or at least equal to Him, in being able to decide for themselves what was good and what was evil. Satan gave seduction his best shot when Jesus was in the wilderness for forty days and nights, preparing for His upcoming ministry.

The devil attempted to seduce Jesus with **physical pleasures** as he painted pictures, perhaps even accompanied by aromas of freshly baked bread before a man who had not eaten in nearly six weeks. *Just a taste! Who would know?*

The devil attempted to seduce Jesus with **spiritual power,** encouraging Him to show off before the religious leaders in Jerusalem by foolishly jumping from the highest point of the Temple and calling on angels to save Him. *Think about how*

---

59   2 Corinthians 11:14
60   2 Thessalonians 2:9b-10

much publicity you will get! You could really have power to preach your messages then!

Finally, the devil attempted to seduce Jesus with **worldly power.** He showed Jesus every kingdom of the world in all their splendor, and offered them to Him. *Just imagine, you would have prestige and authority and respect and influence like no one else. Just do it my way!*

The caveat that was implied in each temptation, but revealed in the final one, was that Jesus would bow down and worship the devil. Notice the progression of the seduction. At first it seems so little, so insignificant (just a *taste* of bread), but the offerings and the consequences escalate. Each time Jesus answered the devil, but not in long dialogue, argument, or discussion. He simply stated the Word of God, and whether the devil liked it or not, there was power in the Word, and he had to back down. [61]

3. Intimidation

When he can't get us to believe his lies, when he can't deceive us, when we know and rely on the Word of God to stand against his seductions, the devil still has a trick up his slimy sleeve. He will attempt to intimidate. This means he does everything he can to make us fearful.

Fear can be paralyzing. Have you ever had such a frightening experience (or anticipated one) that you lost all the good of reason? Maybe you couldn't make yourself call out for help or you were not able to make one foot move in front of the other. You became fear's victim. Many people have dreams about such situations, perhaps symbolizing some inner fears in their lives.

The devil does not inspire the kind of fear that comes

---

61   The Temptation of Jesus is found in Matthew 4:1-11

with awe, reverence, and respect that accompanies a holy fear of the Lord. The devil inspires a fear that causes great anxiety and dread. He delights in painting "worst-case-scenarios" in our minds and bringing obsessive thoughts about death and destruction, humiliation, and ridicule.

Peter discovered this kind of fear and intimidation when Jesus was arrested and brought before the Sanhedrin. In the courtyard with other onlookers, Peter was so overcome with dread that he denied any association with the most important person to him in the whole world. When he realized what he had done, he broke down in deep sorrow and wept. After the resurrection, Jesus' love freed Peter so completely from the effects of this intimidation, that he later contributed powerful truths to the writings of the apostles about living a victorious life, suffering for Christ in joy, being wary of the lies of false prophets, and the joy of perseverance.

John understood the intimidation of the devil, but he, too, had learned from Jesus about how to stand against its effects. *"There is no fear in love. But perfect love drives out fear, because fear has to do with punishment. The one who fears is not made perfect in love."*[62]

Paul said, *"For God did not give us a spirit of fear, but a spirit of power, of love and of self-discipline."*[63]

All the weapons that Satan aims at us are puny in power compared to the stronghold of Christ. If we listen to the voice of Jesus more clearly and heed His warnings, we can avoid the grazes and even the piercings of Satan's arrows. A big reason why

---

62   1 John 4:18
63   2 Timothy 1:7

the devil's voice can be so loud in our ears, and even so appealing at times, is because we choose to engage in his activities. Occult practices will cloud the Spirit of God. Drugs will cloud the will to choose God. Ungodly relationships will cloud the cleansing of purity and holiness. Sinful attitudes of the heart will cloud the love relationship with Christ. These are all voluntary willful acts we might choose to pursue. But involvement in any of them puts blinders on our spiritual eyes and stops up our spiritual ears, so that the presence and voice of God seems very remote.

In no way is God's power diminished when this happens. Rather, a smoke screen is erected and we put up obstacles in our lives that make it very difficult to find Him.

These are obvious ways in which we lose our ways from God's will. But there are less obvious ways the devil will draw us away from God if he can. He does not play fair, and he will use anything he can.

We can become accustomed to life-long fear through close brushes with death, especially if such things happen to us as children. We can be drawn into a pattern of generational sin before we have the maturity to recognize its source. We can repeat actions that displease God until habitual sin becomes a way of life and we no longer recognize it as such. Many of these things may occur before we come to Christ. Or, even after coming to Christ, we can assume a ritual of religiosity in our lives that inhibits intimate relationship with God.

Satan may or may not introduce such situations into our lives, but he will most assuredly use them to his advantage if we don't confess them, renounce them, and allow the Blood of Jesus to cleanse us.

Antidotes to the World, the Flesh, and the Devil

An antidote is generally thought of as a medicine given to counteract poison. It can also be whatever it takes to counteract the evil which something else might produce.[64] There are Godly antidotes to any of the influences of the world, the flesh and the devil that are more than able to free us from their clutches and the effects of their voices ringing in our ears.

Antidote #1: Jesus is Lord

The most basic, and I hope the most obvious, antidote is to believe in and trust in God through a relationship with Jesus His Son. I have learned in our ministry to never take for granted with **any** group of people that all are born again. Belonging to a church, ministering in a church, professionally serving the Lord in any capacity, praying well-articulated prayers, being a "Christian counselor," and even more accomplishments never guarantee one the empowerment that is promised to believers. This empowerment only comes by being born again, having the Spirit of God within, and enjoying the effects of His resurrection life in your life!

It is surprising how many people in the above categories have never in fact cemented their relationship with Christ through actually confessing their sins, intentionally receiving God's forgiveness, genuinely believing in their heart and publicly confessing with their mouth that He is Lord. People can easily

---

64   Definition from the *American Dictionary of the English Language*, Noah Webster, 1828

slide into a role in a church or embrace a theological doctrine or find a Christian group to join that is much like a club. Publicly declaring one's heart, along with the witness of others through prayer, really does make a difference. Without such tangible evidence we will harbor an inroad of doubt in our life. This is why testimony is so vital to overcome the devil. It's not just the testimony of what God has done for you that is important, but the testimony of your heart, your belief, of yielding your will to the will of God.

"Submit yourselves, then, to God. Resist the devil, and he will flee from you. Come near to God and He will come near to you." (James 4:7-8a)

Antidote #2: *The Power of Holy Spirit*

Jesus never intended that His disciples foray out on missions into the world to spread the gospel unless they were empowered to stand against the enemies of God. He specifically asked them to wait until the Spirit came as a gift from the Father to indwell them. They first experienced this at Pentecost. It was much more than a Spiritually high experience. It was a necessity for ministry and survival. His empowerment is just as vital to us today!

The power of Holy Spirit constantly reminds us when we sin, convicts us so we can confess and be forgiven, and enables us to stay pure before a holy God.

The power of Holy Spirit binds our hearts to God so that we might maintain a personal relationship with Him, being drawn deeper and deeper into His healing love.

The power of Holy Spirit shows us how to pray, translates God's language to our hearts, and intercedes for us in ways that words cannot express.

The power of Holy Spirit gives us the armor that protects us from God's enemies.

"You will receive power when the Holy Spirit comes upon you." (Acts 1:8)

Antidote #3: Renunciation

To renounce something is to declare it null and void in the Name of Jesus, and then follow up your declaration with deliberate actions. Some Christian traditions incorporate this kind of renunciation in their baptismal services. It doesn't have to be that formal. It is an intention of the heart.

*In the Name of Jesus **I renounce the influence of the world** in my life! I ask You to show me areas where I am following the prince of the world rather than the Prince of Peace. I ask for Your power to stand against the world's values and to embrace the values of God.*

*In the Name of Jesus **I renounce the influence of my unhealed being – the flesh**. I submit myself to You, the Healer of my mind, my emotions, and my body. I want to collaborate with You as You bring wholeness to me. Show me where to begin and I will follow You.*

*In the Name of Jesus **I renounce the influence of the devil** in my life. I confess my sins and receive Your forgiveness so that I may be set free from his claims on my life. I will wear Your truth, salvation, righteousness, peace, and faith, and the Word of God – the armor You provide for me against Satan's wiles.*

When any of these voices come to me again, I will recognize them, and hang up!

There will be no conversation, no dialogue, no discussion. Just simply: **Not interested!**

If you deliberately renounced the voices opposing
God in your life, make it real in several ways:

Declare it in your heart
Speak it with your voice
Write it in your Journal
Tell someone what you did

Go back to this renunciation many times in your Journal,
letting God refresh it and empower you to
continue walking in your declaration.

CHAPTER 21
PAST TENSE – FUTURE PERFECT

There is an old saying that "You are who your father says you are."

I believe this with all my heart. I am growing into the woman God created me to be by listening to my heavenly Father's voice and letting Him give me my true identity. He's told me some very positive things about myself I had trouble believing at first. But, over the years, as I spend time with Him, believe His Word, and write the personal words He has for me in my Listening Prayer Journal, my transformation has increased.

If your earthly father has been a cheerleader for you, affirming you, spending time with you, encouraging you, and telling you he is proud of you, then, you have an identity that reflects his words. What a blessing! His words to you over the years have made you secure in your masculinity as a man, or your femininity as a woman. His words have given you a sense of confidence and security that have enabled you to do meaningful things without fear of failure and fear of disappointing others. He modeled for you what God, your heavenly Father, wants to do every day of your life.

If you grew up in such a family where encouragement and affirmation were normal, you probably don't think about it very much. Being comfortable in your own skin just feels natural to you. You probably take for granted that you can relate to others in healthy ways and that you are not occupied with feelings of self-consciousness, inadequacy, and inferiority.

Transforming the Lack

But if your growing-up years were punctuated by harsh, critical words, demeaning threats, or being ignored, you carry these words and attitudes with you every day. They color every relationship you have, and they greatly influence the way you view yourself. This can affect you all your life – *until God's words to you replace the old ones!* Then the transformation begins!

An example: Silvie had never heard her father say to her, "I love you." Those became the magical, illusive three words she longed to hear all her life. As soon as she was aware of the ways she could attract boys, she began to throw away her dignity, her modesty, and her innocence just to hear those three words, or to experience some demonstration of them. But, her emptiness within only increased. With a wake of ruined relationships in her life she came to Conlee and me for healing prayer.

The prayer time was simple. She didn't need to tell her long, sordid story. She didn't need counseling. She didn't need compassion. *She needed to hear God!* For years she had been told, "God loves you and He has a plan for your life." That was true, but hearing the truth from others didn't change her, until it was applied by God Himself. For Silvie, it was as though that truth was reserved for every other person but herself.

We prayed for her: *Lord, enlarge Silvie's capacity to hear Your voice. Still the voices of the past, fill the voids of words never spoken, and let her hear what You are saying to her in this moment.* Then we waited. All she needed was a little encouragement and to be surrounded by the faith that God would speak to her heart. And you can imagine what she heard. God said to her in her heart, *Silvie, I love you!*

You could see her countenance change as the words began to resonate throughout her whole being. But then, just as quickly, her look darkened to skepticism. "I just made that up. It was just what I wanted to hear."

"Of course, you wanted to hear it!" we both exclaimed at the same time. "You've wanted to hear that you are loved all your life. God has always known what you wanted and was waiting for you to hear it from Him. Why would He say something to you that wasn't true? He put the desire to be loved in you when you were born, and He is going to continue to love you day after day, telling you who you are and that you have worth."

One word from God can change a life! (Well, in Silvie's case it was actually three words). Later, out of knowing she was loved by God and internalizing His love, she was able to do the work of forgiving her parents, confessing her sins of seeking love in wrong ways, and receiving God's forgiveness. Over time, she began to have her innocence restored. (Yes, God can really do that!) She received a child-like trust in God and in others, believing that she had value and could glorify God in her life.

Hearing God speak three words to her heart was only the beginning for Silvie. But it was a vital beginning. Without those words coming alive within her, she would always doubt and tend to revert to old patterns of behavior and ways of relating to others.

Parts of Silvie's story could easily have been my own story. Perhaps you identify with parts of it, too. I didn't throw my innocence away with men, but I was desperate for affirmation in other ways. I felt that I must over-achieve to win the approval of others. Yet, I always questioned every good thing said to me or said about me. No compliment was satisfying. There was never enough to make up for the void of hearing my father's affirming words. And I was always anticipating the criticism which I thought I deserved.

When nothing is said to you at all by your father, you can feel as though there is nothing of value in you to be affirmed. When you are called demeaning or embarrassing names by your father, they stick like glue. When either one of these situations is part of your past, you can actually get to the point where you are afraid to hear what God will say to you. *What if He says the same things my father did? What if that is who I really am? Or, what if He says nothing to me at all?* It can feel like it's easier not to listen to God.

Help Wanted

When we first met Silvie, she didn't know she needed to hear God. She didn't know what she needed. She just wanted help. The circumstances of her past were defining her much more than anything else. Fortunately, her pain overcame her pride, and she finally cried out. The whole process of coming free from her past was much less painful than she thought it would be. And just like forgetting the pain of childbirth, the joy of her new life quickly erased the embarrassment and reluctance she felt when she first became vulnerable.

When I first started listening to God, I needed help, too. Conlee became my first listening prayer partner. We began to share with one another the things God spoke to our hearts. It helped me to bring what was buried in my heart to the light, out of my circular thinking, and into conversation. We still do this together. I can see much more objectively when I discuss things with him, and will often receive further insight through his observations. We have always encouraged one another to keep on listening to God, to keep asking God questions for clarification, and to continue being vulnerable with Him and with one another.

Not every married couple is able to do this together. It was difficult for us when we first began. It was a huge leap of faith to begin to be **totally** honest with my husband. We had some rocky beginnings learning how to become vulnerable with one another, but we persevered.

Soon after we were born again and began listening to God, we became aware that we were praying with Leanne, praying with our little group that was forming, praying by ourselves, but not praying together as husband and wife and parents of two boys. We were familiar with the saying that was on many billboards, "The family that prays together stays together." So, it just seemed like a good thing for us to start doing that.

We had no one else to initiate this new activity for us. We were on our own. Prior to our commitment to Jesus, we never prayed at home, only in corporate prayers in church. Sometimes we said a blessing before a meal, but that was usually only when we had guests for some strange reason. It just was not something we felt to be meaningful or comfortable doing within the confines of our family of four.

So, when Conlee and I made the decision to pray together, we had no idea how to do it. Suddenly, it seemed as if we were about to do the most revolutionary thing we had ever done. It is hard to describe how uncomfortable and vulnerable I felt even just discussing it with him. Maybe the following description of our preparations will give you some idea.

> We set a date. On Thursday night, **after the boys were asleep**, we would pray together. *Where should we do it? Downstairs? Upstairs in our bedroom?* We decided to be in our bedroom. *Do we sit? Stand? Kneel?* We decided to kneel. *On opposite sides of the bed? The same side of the bed?* We decided on the same side. *With lights on? Lights off? A candle?* We decided on one lamp, no candle. *With praise music on? No music?* We decided on no music. *Would Conlee begin? Would I?* We decided Conlee would pray first.

During all these deliberations which took hours, my heart was pounding. I wasn't this nervous on my wedding night! I was exposing a part of myself to my husband that had never been exposed before. My soul was going to be wide open before God, Conlee, and myself. Our relationship would change. I could have no secrets. Prayer was a serious thing. I could withhold a part of myself in conversation with my husband, but when God was involved, I could no longer do that. My expectations were huge!

And so, on Thursday night, after the boys were sleeping,

kneeling beside me on the same side of the bed with one lamp on and no praise music, Conlee began to pray to God, our first prayer together. And this is exactly what he prayed:

Dear Lord, please make Signa a better wife!

I nearly died! To me, it was as if he had stabbed me in the heart, totally deflating my huge balloon of expectation. Of course, I wasn't just hearing what he later described as praying "the desire of his heart," but I was hearing words of my past that had been indelibly imprinted on my soul. *You are not good enough. You are not acceptable. You are inferior.* My response was to run from the room in tears, leaving our first experiment with family prayer in shambles.

So, when I say that we got off to a rocky start as listening prayer partners, I'm not exaggerating. It didn't come naturally to either of us. I don't know why I ever expected it would because we were entering into a supernatural realm. The kind of prayer that connects us with God's heart is greater than any conversation in the world. When we pray, something happens beyond our scope of normal experience. Prayer changes us!

The unexpected, disappointing results of our first prayer together that night opened me up to begin to receive a deep healing from the wounds of my past. Only God could have done that! Conlee could have told me repeatedly that I had difficulties accepting myself, and believing I had worth, and on and on. But I would never have let him go there with me. It was too painful and embarrassing to contemplate. I wanted, instead, to ignore my past, never bring it to the light. But God in an instant exposed my heart. Yes, it was painful. Yes, I tried to hide. Yes, at first I blamed Conlee. But God spoke to me through my pain. He brought it right to the surface, and **in the pain,** He began to show me that He loved me beyond imagination and was beginning my healing process.

Although it was incredibly awkward, our first prayer together was amazingly successful. It surely wasn't what I expected, but it was exactly what God used to break through the vulnerability barriers Conlee and I had with one another and with God. I began my journey to wholeness. Our marriage took on a new level of honesty and openness. The wounds of my past were being transformed. Amazingly, God answered Conlee's prayer! I became a better wife.

A Crucible

Marriage is a great crucible for spiritual growth. A crucible is a place or a set of circumstances where people or things are subjected to forces that test them and often bring change. But, with marriage partners timing is vital. You can't rush one another or force the other to grow out of season. Marriage partners may be at different stages of their spiritual growth and maturity. They may have trust issues with one another, or they just may not be ready yet to be that spiritually vulnerable. (Conlee and I had already been married for over ten years when we first prayed together!)

Asking God to bring **someone** into your life as a listening prayer partner is a good prayer. It doesn't even have to be someone you know all that well. Just pray for someone who loves to spend time with God in prayer, someone who will be honest with you, and someone who can be trusted. Trust is essential!

Many early morning men's groups meet this purpose for

those who gather. We know of several men who gather for coffee before work two or three times a month to discuss a Christian book they are all reading. Or, they might do a Bible Study together, or they might share their lives and pray for one another. But, at some point if they develop a trust relationship with one another, they can begin to share what God is saying to them. Through His words, each one will be encouraged, both to hear God for himself and to bless his brothers. Men tend to tell it like it is and be honest with one another when that trust level is established.

Women's groups, whether just two people or larger, seem to form more easily than men's. Women are usually more relational and have less trouble sharing their feelings and needs with one another. But to be honest, this very quality can get in the way of a good, listening prayer partner relationship. If God speaks to me about something and I need an objective prayer partner who can help me sort it out, I want to hear what God is telling her, not her human compassion, understanding, or attitude of "I want you to feel good."

I need a prayer partner who will be truthful with me if she senses a red flag about a way I have interpreted what I hear from God. I need her to guide me back to Scripture when I let my feelings or experiences get in the way. I need her to exhort me in love and encourage me when I get lazy. This is hard for most women. We want people to like us when we are with them. We might speak very forthrightly about someone who is not present, but face-to-face, we tend to say what will make someone feel good in the moment. This attitude does not promote wholeness.

Exhortation

Many times I heard Leanne say, "Everyone loves an exhorter." I would argue with her over and over. "No, they don't! We hate to be exhorted!" I had to learn what true exhortation is. I was equating it with criticism, someone trying to force me to do something I didn't want to do, or being scolded. Instead, I found that when a person exhorts me the way God does, I am encouraged, cheered on, set on the right path, and persuaded to move to a higher level. This is love!

Unfortunately, we tend to ignore the necessity of exhortation in our lives. It is so high above jealousy which wants me to fail or envy which wants me to lose whatever is good. Exhortation lifts us to higher places. We need exhorters who will be our biggest cheerleaders. I need a listening prayer partner who will not be reluctant to call me to a higher place and speak truth into my life.

Worship

Often the most essential ingredient for any listening prayer group or listening prayer partner relationship is missing. It is worship! Calling upon the Name of Jesus and praying together is great, but purposefully spending time together in adoration and thanksgiving for who He is and what He does opens the doors to intimacy with Him and the fullest awareness of His presence in the conversation that follows. When worship is missing, the time of sharing can often devolve into a gossipy time of talking about too many personal details of one's life, and leaving a sense of incompleteness and emptiness, perhaps even embarrassment, after the group disperses. Instead, one should expect to leave each session of listening prayer with a greater sense of God's presence, encouragement, and blessing. Worship takes us there.

Redeeming the Past through Vulnerability

That important first year of my new Christian life, I would ask Leanne a hundred questions a day. She never seemed to tire in her quest to disciple me. If I asked her something she didn't know, she would say, "I'll pray about that and let you know." And she would! I knew I was receiving God's wisdom through her, not just her own wisdom and experience.

One day when I requested, "Teach me how to hear God," she immediately asked me a question. "What is the desire of your heart?"

At first I had no idea what that had to do with listening to God, but rather than explain it to me, she just said, "Don't analyze it or decide what your desires **should** be. Just let them come up and then write them in your Journal. God will show you your primary one and what He wants to deal with."

This wasn't as easy for me as you might think. I knew this wasn't a "Miss America question" that required a "Miss America answer" (we **all** want world peace!). This was more than that. It was very personal. Perhaps something I had never told anyone, ever. Perhaps something I didn't even know was in me.

The first few desires that came up seemed to be very self-centered. I wanted to cram them back down, but I began to write down everything that started to bubble to the surface. There were many layers of desires. I realized some of them had been with me since childhood. How was I supposed to narrow it down to just one? *The desire of my heart.*

Aha! Jesus is in my heart. He knows what is there. I can ask Him! And so I did. Simple as that. He showed me my primary desire and it was amazing. Leanne knew what she was talking about. Getting in touch with my desires really had led me to listen to God and hear what He was saying. Until He revealed it, the main, over-riding desire of my heart was hidden from me because it was so familiar. I never thought of it as a desire at all, only as a void in my life.

I looked in my Bible and found several scriptures about desires. Here are only a few:

"May He give you the desire of your heart and make all your plans succeed." (Psalm 20:4)

"Hope deferred makes the heart sick, but a longing fulfilled is a tree of life." (Proverbs 13:12)

"Blessed are those who hunger and thirst for righteousness, for they will be filled." (Matthew 5:6)

I saw in the Bible how God would often multiply the desires of one's heart when they were in His will. When Solomon asked God for wisdom, God said,

> *"Since this is your heart's desire and you have not asked for wealth, riches or honor, nor for the death of your enemies, and since you have not asked for a long life but for wisdom and knowledge to govern My people over whom*

I have made you king, therefore wisdom and knowledge will be given you. And I will also give you wealth, riches and honor, such as no king who was before you ever had and none after you will have." (2 Chronicles 1:10-12)

I was beginning to feel more comfortable doing this. It lined up with the Word of God, so obviously God wants us to desire in our hearts and He wants us to know what those desires are.

And then God said to me, *Now that you know what the deepest desire of your heart is, will you give it to Me?*

I hesitated. I was learning to trust God but I had just gotten in touch with something so primal inside me that I felt like I would lose my identity if I gave it away. This desire had kept me on course all my life. *What would He do with it? Why would He want it?* To think about giving this to God was the most vulnerable thing I had ever done, even more vulnerable than praying with Conlee the first time. I had to really trust to give this into someone's care, not knowing if I would be criticized, ridiculed, laughed at, ignored - or what.

I thought of Abraham when God asked if he would give up the most precious possession in the world to him - his son, Isaac. God honored Abraham's sacrificial gift by handing him back the life of his son.

Finally . . . *Oh God. I give it to you. I willingly hand You the desire of my heart that has been in me as long as I have been alive. It is Yours. It is my sacrifice to You. You are going to have to show me how to live without it.*

Leanne had impressed upon me that when you give God something, it is always important to watch to see what He does with it, and to listen to hear what He says about it. So I waited.

I sensed that God kissed what I placed in His hands and then He blessed it. He multiplied it by the blessing, and then He placed that desire back into my heart. Only now, it had a totally different feel. It was no longer the hope for something never met, it was the sense of a solid center of fulfillment.

The Desire of My Heart

What I gave to God was my life-long desire to be loveable. I had never experienced "loveable" before. My husband would tell me how much he loved me and I never quite believed him. There was always the latent sense of guilt that I wasn't doing enough, wasn't pretty enough, or didn't deserve to be loved. Although we had a good marriage, there was always that whisper of undercurrent that kept the intimacy from being what it could be. There was always the sense that a friend would reject me, that even my own child might decide he did not really love me. I had grown used to that feeling. I coped well. But I wasn't whole. I didn't know how to put all my weight down on my true self.

When God showed me the desire of my heart, and empowered me to give it to Him, He replaced the desire with much more than a deep sense of being loved by Him. He actually redeemed the years of rejection and loneliness and sense of inadequacy. *He became in me the love I always wanted,* and the result was that His love changed the ways I looked at the world around me. His love in me changed our marriage, the way I mothered my children, the ways I related to friends and strangers. His love in me drove out fears and hesitations that had kept me from living life in its fullest.

It all came from giving Him that deepest desire I thought no one – not even God – would ever know about. And now, I'm writing about it in a book for all to read! This is the result of hearing His voice speak to me in the shadows of my life, bringing all things into His light, and receiving His deep healing. As the man said who wrote me the letter about his wife, *What if I had not been listening?* It's not so much a question, as an expression of awe at what God will accomplish in your life when you hear His voice.

Serendipity

Becoming used to being "loveable" was quite a journey! I hadn't realized how much that latent sense of being "un-loveable" had colored my life. I realized there had been labels, or code words attached to the old un-loveable feelings. Those labels and old codes had to go. They could pop up in the most unexpected ways, bringing up the past as though the miracle of God's love hadn't happened to me.

So, once again, sitting with my Bible and my journal, I listened to God. *What are those labels that jerk me back to the times when I felt so un-loveable?*

First, He showed me that there had been nicknames. When I heard them or even thought about them, I would cringe inside although I thought there was no outward sign of what I felt. One that came up first was the nickname my father had for me most of my childhood: *Butch.* I wrote it in my Journal. Just looking at it in my handwriting gave me the oddest sense of discontent. I never wanted to be my daddy's "Butch." I was his only child. I wanted to be his princess, his darling, his baby girl. But I was labeled "Butch" and it stuck. It stuck not only in ways that kept it repeated, but it stuck in my heart. That label diminished my sense of femininity and loveliness. If a father's words tell us who we are, that word told me that I was un-loveable as a daughter and I believed that everyone else saw me in the same way.

I asked God to exchange "Butch" for the name He had for me. Immediately, I heard, *Beloved.* Then, came such a surge of words from God that I was writing as fast as I could. *Precious, Beautiful, Darling, Princess, Prized one, Lovely, Graceful, ...* It went on and on. I gave God that one word from my youth that had defined me more than it should, and He gave me back endless words of affirmation and love and truth from His perspective. I was finally hearing from my Father who I am!

At another listening time, He asked me to give Him my **family motto.** *We didn't have one. What are You asking? Is it like a family crest?*

He began to show me that the motto of a family is the unwritten set of rules they live by. The rules may be unspoken but they underlie every aspect of the family's life together. Again, I needed Him to show me what it had been in my family. Whatever it had been, I was so used to it I could not objectively define it. But, while listening to Him, I saw it! He showed me a picture in my imagination. It was the image of a framed needlepoint of something so entrenched in our family that we observed it, didn't question it, but never spoke it. Although, it was never actually put in writing or needlepoint, it was indelibly engraved on each of us:

What happens in the family stays in the family.

Another homespun way to say this is a saying my mother spoke often, "Don't air your dirty laundry for all to see." Although there were some really dreadful things that happened in our family of three behind closed doors, they were never discussed with anyone outside the home. For the first time I began to wonder why I had never told my grandmother, whom I adored, what was happening. Why didn't I go to a pastor, teacher, or close friend? Instead, I acted as though everything was normal, although it was far from that.

God said to me, *I am going to give you a new motto for your present family!* Intuitively, I knew what it would be about but it was vague, until once when we were in a dusty, little antique shop in Rothenburg, Germany. I saw the motto, hand-carved on a little wooden plaque, in German. I would have bought it at any cost, because God told me on the spot that it was meant for our family. However, it was ridiculously inexpensive. In fact, the owner tried to give it to me, saying he didn't think it was at all valuable. But I wanted to pay the price for it just like Abraham wanted to pay for the land at Machpelah[65] or David wanted to pay for the threshing floor on which the Temple would one day be built.[66]

The plaque with our family motto for which I paid only a few euro is now in our home. It says:

Ich und mein Haus wollen dem Herrn dienen.

I love it! It declares that for me and my family, we will

---

65   Genesis 23
66   2 Samuel 24:18-25

serve the Lord!

Several years ago at one of our monthly *Journey* team meetings, I shared about the importance of knowing one's childhood family motto and how it might carry over to our present families. I asked them to pray, asking God to show them what mottos they grew up with. When everyone began to share, it was as revealing and healing to each of them as it had been to me.

One woman said her family motto had always been, *Every day is a good day!* Most of us thought this sounded wonderful. Imagine growing up in a family that optimistic! However, she said it was such a strong influence in the family that no one had permission to demonstrate a genuine emotion that was not superficially cheerful. Acceptable outward appearances had the utmost importance. She discovered how damaging this was when her first baby died shortly after his birth. Her family did not grieve the loss with her and did not give her the liberty to grieve outwardly. Everyone acted as though it never happened, as though the child had never been conceived. It took many years and much healing from God before she was able to genuinely grieve the loss of her first child. That night at the *Journey* team meeting, when God showed her the childhood family motto, she saw the foundation of much of her previous pain. God had already given her a new motto for her family and she shared it with much authentic joy: *Restoration!*

What is the desire of your heart?
What are the labels of your past that continue to define you?
What was the motto of your family home?
What is the motto of your life today?
Write all these in your Listening Prayer Journal!

CHAPTER 22

A MATTER OF TASTE

There are so many powerful examples in the Bible of how a personal word from God can change a life, a nation, and the world. I am overwhelmed with the realization that one message from God spoken to a single person who listens and heeds His words can accomplish what governments and armies cannot. I thought of Abraham, Moses, Joseph (Jacob's son), Daniel, Jeremiah, Joseph (Jesus' adopted father), Paul, and so many others. But the one God wants me to focus on right now is Ezekiel. And the specific focal point out of the life-time of this great God-listener is found in Ezekiel 2-3.

God took me on quite a circuitous route to get me to this story. It is all part of a conversation He and I shared. This will, perhaps, give you some insight into how I listen to God and allow Him to take me on journeys when we have our conversation quiet times together.

For several years I managed a catering business called "A Matter of Taste." It was already named that when I went to work there. To be honest the name had to grow on me. At first I thought it vaguely implied that not everyone would love the food we prepared. But the more I thought about it, the more I realized that if we could just get people to taste something they thought they didn't like, our food was so great they would love it and order more. We watched this happen many times.

We not only catered parties, weddings and special events, we had a take-out shop, primarily for people who didn't want to cook or were too busy. Many harried mothers dropped by every afternoon after carpool to pick up "home-cooked" meals for their families. We would encourage them to try new things they never thought their family would eat. For instance women who said their husbands or children hated spinach would be encouraged to taste our delicious Spinach Madeleine and take home a small container for a trial. Invariably, they would begin to order it every week. It really was a matter of their tasting and finding it delicious.

God initiated this principle. Through His psalmist, David, God said, *"Taste and see that the Lord is good."* [67] Even if you have grown up believing that there are certain things about God that just aren't for you, things you don't want to be a part of, things you are not interested in, and places in the Kingdom you have decided you will not go - God may be saying to you, *Just taste. You don't have to clean your plate. Just take one bite.* We say that to our children all the time!

When we first got married, Conlee told me he didn't like casseroles of any kind. I couldn't imagine this. I had grown up on casseroles in my family. But he insisted he would not eat any variety of meat, vegetables and sauce mixed together. They all

---

67   Psalm 34:8a

had to be separate on the plate. To me that was boring. So I began to experiment. I cooked various combinations of interesting ingredients for him but I didn't call them casseroles. I called them "surprises." I asked him just to taste and see. He really was surprised because he found out he actually liked most of them. After a while some of them became his favorites and he even requested them. When I eventually asked him which casseroles he had eaten as a child that he hated so much, he replied that he had never eaten casseroles. His mother never made them!

How This Relates to Ezekiel[68]

Ezekiel spent a lot of time with God even though he lived in exile in a foreign country. Circumstances weren't great, but God was with him. In prayer he had visions of God, of heaven, of spiritual creatures, of glory unimaginable. His response to such visions was to fall on his face before God in awe. He would just listen. It must have been overwhelming.

On one occasion, while Ezekiel was facedown in awe, basking in the presence of the Lord, the Spirit raised him to his feet and gave him a very strange assignment. He was going to be sent back to his homeland, to Israel. But God told him that the Israelites he would find there were rebellious, revolting against God, obstinate and stubborn. They had grown hard against God, and yet, in His continuing love for them, God was going to send a prophet to speak His words so that they would repent. That prophet would be Ezekiel.

God did not paint a pretty picture of what Ezekiel would

_____
68   All references are from Ezekiel 2-3.

find in Israel, and He did not whitewash the assignment. He told Ezekiel that his countrymen would be like briers, thorns, and scorpions to him. The Israelites would not like the words God gave him to tell them. They might even refuse to listen. It would be dangerous. But God told Ezekiel to speak His words whether the people listened or not.

Would you want to receive such an assignment? No doubt, Ezekiel was reluctant to say the least. But God gave him a symbol of the empowerment that would be upon him to accomplish the seemingly impossible task. God showed him a scroll. On both sides of it were written horrible, sorrowful words of lament and mourning. It described death. It was the worst thing one could imagine. Surely, this scroll would do nothing to encourage Ezekiel to take the assignment.

Yet, God told him to *taste it, eat it! Put it in your mouth and swallow it!* Who would want to put something so disgusting in his mouth?

But Ezekiel had seen visions of God. He had been in His awesome presence. He had heard God's voice. He knew Him. He could trust Him. And so, he obeyed Him. He actually ate the disgusting words of the scroll.

Amazingly, as he did so, *it tasted as sweet as honey in his mouth!*

The lesson we learn from Ezekiel is that no matter how difficult it is to comprehend situations, how hard it seems to digest facts, how painful life appears to be, how impossible a task seems to fulfill, when we allow the words of God to be a part of us, to penetrate our lives, He can turn them into something that brings life and sweetness. Although what He speaks to me today may *seem* unappetizing, even impossible, if I just *taste* it instead of discarding it, I may discover an amazing sweetness to life that I never expected.

A Personal Tasting

In the summer of 1977, Conlee and I, with our three sons, were on the Gulf Coast for our annual two week beach vacation. We looked forward to this time every year, enjoying the water, the sand, the fun activities, and especially the church we attended while there. We had been committed to Jesus for several years by this time, were happily serving Him in many capacities, were growing in the ministry of healing prayer, were teaching small groups, and we were thoroughly enjoying the success of Conlee's expanding mechanical contracting business.

However, there was one big frustration in our lives. We had such large visions for ministry, for seeing people become whole, and for being a part of a congregation who would radical-ly obey God. As much as we loved our new pastors, we couldn't seem to find a leader who had the same passion for bringing such a ministry of wholeness into his church. This was especially frus-trating for Conlee who was in lay leadership.

The reason why we so loved to visit the church at the beach each summer was that the ministry of wholeness for God's people was their priority. They had a freedom in the Spirit in worship, and we always received such a spiritual renewal in our lives each time we were there.

This particular summer had been an ideal vacation for each of us. A couple of nights before we were to return home I was sitting in the living room of our rented condo working on a needlepoint I wanted to finish as a memento of our holiday. It was late, everyone else was fast asleep, and it was wonderfully quiet. I was just about to put my needlework away and head for bed when I heard God speak to me in an unmistakable way. It wasn't audible, but it was such an intense impression there was no doubt it was God. I knew I had not thought up such a thing. *You are going to be a pastor's wife.* I was stunned. I heard it three times, the intensity increasing each time. *You are going to be a pastor's wife. You are going to be a pastor's wife.*

This word was so unexpected, so undesired, so foreign to anything I had ever thought about, and so far from any conversation Conlee and I had ever had, that my first thought was fearful. *Oh, no! God is telling me that Conlee is going to die and I will marry a pastor!* My heart was pounding with the revelation and with the interpretation I had given to it. But, as I was trained to do, I got my Listening Prayer Journal, wrote it down exactly as I heard it without my interpretation, and dated the entry.

When I went to bed that night, I couldn't sleep because of all the thoughts whirling around in my head. *I don't want to be a pastor's wife. I have watched so many of them lose their identity. They are criticized over every little thing; their families are put under a microscope. They are expected to behave in certain ways. Lord, I am just beginning to get whole and discover the woman You created me to be. I don't want to lose my true self in some expectations a church would have for me.* On and on the circular thoughts went, long into the night. I knew I could never tell Conlee about this. And so, I didn't.

But I thought about it many times. Over the years, I attempted to make it fit into several situations that occurred. Conlee taught a Sunday School class. *This is sort of like being a pastor, isn't it?* Conlee was elected to the governing board of the church. *Surely, that's like a lay pastor.* Conlee led a prayer group. *That's pastoring people in a way, just not full time.* Repeatedly, I rationalized the word from God. Meanwhile, the healing God was doing in both of us was increasing and we were maturing spiritually in many ways.

Exactly three years later, our family was once again on vacation in the same Gulf Coast spot. We arrived late on Saturday night, and although we were tired from the long drive, we wanted to be in the church we loved so much on Sunday morning. Getting three boys up and dressed early for church on their first day of vacation wasn't easy, and so, of course we were late. Many tourists joined that local congregation during the summer months, and folding chairs were added in every available space to accommodate the crowd. An usher set up chairs for us in the last possible space in the very back of the packed out church, and I was aware that Conlee was having a difficult time relaxing. He had driven for two days, he had unpacked the motor home, gone to the grocery store, and had very little sleep. Besides that, he had been helping to corral three sons that morning, was upset that we were late, bothered that we couldn't see or hear very well from where we were sitting, and it was really, really hot. However, he was wrestling with something far more important, that he only told me about later.

In the Ring with Jesus

For two days, during the long hours behind the isolated

driver's seat of the RV, Conlee had been in a silent wrestling match with the Lord. It had been eight years since we had committed ourselves to Jesus. Our lives and our priorities for our family had changed drastically. We were seeing many other lives changed as we prayed with people. The opportunities for ministry were infinite. We had joined a believing church, and although we loved our pastors, they didn't seem called to the same mission we were. They supported us, but were often reluctant to over-ride tradition when God would initiate something new. It was extremely frustrating. At one point in this wrestling match, Conlee even told God, *Lord, if You show me where to go, I'll even move, change churches, start over somewhere else. Just lead me to a church that is committed to do what You want, no matter what!* God seemed silent to his pleas.

All of this was marinating inside Conlee as he sat on the back row in the hot, crowded church, not able to see or hear well, and with three fidgety sons who would rather be on the beach. We looked forward to being here all year, and it was not turning out to be a very spiritual time. Because he couldn't really participate well in the service from our vantage point, he took up his ongoing complaint with God that had been left unresolved. *Lord, what are You going to do with us? I am just looking for that spiritual leader who will have the same visions we have!*

And then he heard God speak for the first time on this matter. *Conlee, are you willing to be that leader?* This was a wrestling hold he didn't know how to counteract. *Oh, Lord, I didn't mean that! I'm serving you as a business man. I am willing to serve in a lot of leadership positions, but not as the pastoral leader of a church. I can't do that.* This conversation with God went on for the rest of the two hour service.

There was Holy Communion that Sunday. Everyone was ushered, row by row, to the front of the church to kneel to receive the bread and the wine. Now, nearly two hours after we arrived at the church, we were finally able to go forward to participate. It was nearly over.

Our family of five knelt together. The pastor walked along in front of us, placing a piece of the communion bread in each outstretched hand. He was a sweet, gentle, Godly man who blessed us every summer when we attended his church. We never had a personal conversation with him over the years, but we always admired the way he listened to God, and carefully chose his words to convey truth. He was obviously well-loved by his congregation. We respected him from afar.

He placed the bread in Conlee's hands, then mine, then our oldest son's. Then he stopped and turned back to Conlee. He stood there for a moment and said quietly, "I believe God has given me a word for you today. May I share it with you?"

How would you ever decline such an invitation? Even though by this time Conlee was really upset with God, totally shocked over what God had just asked him about leading a church, and still physically and mentally worn out from the on-going wrestling match, he nodded. The pastor conveyed these words from God.

"God has opened a door for you this morning that surprised you. Yet, it is one you have been looking for with all your heart. Your fears and reservations about walking through that door are fears from the enemy, not from God. If you want to find the peace you are searching for, you will walk through the door."

With that, the pastor calmly walked on, distributing the bread, unaware of the earthquake just released in our family. My heart nearly stopped! I heard it all and I **knew** what this meant. But I couldn't say a thing. This was between Conlee and God.

When we left the church, walking to the crowded parking lot, all Conlee said was, "We have to talk!"

It was much later that afternoon before we had a chance to be alone. The boys had worn themselves out at the beach and the pool, had been fed and were in the condo reading. We walked on the beach at sunset and Conlee told me everything I just shared with you. I had no idea he had been that frustrated for so long. After baring his heart and soul to me, he finally said, "What do **you** think about all this?" He fully expected me to be his ally in refusing God's offer.

I just took his hand and said, "Let's go back to the condo. I want to show you something." I showed him my journal, dated **exactly** three years before. *You are going to be a pastor's wife.*

Conlee went to seminary in 1984, and was ordained to full-time ministry in 1987. Serving in this kind of ministry has been the joy of our lives!

I hope you can see how giving just a "taste" of the future was God's loving way of preparing my heart for what would bring us both fulfillment. I wish you could know how, over time, the taste became so sweet that we ate completely the feast He prepared for us, and we were more than satisfied. We were being completed. He answered the desires of our hearts. And it wasn't just for us, but for the many who find healing in their lives as we minister to them.

You have no idea how the one taste God gives you today will be a banquet for you and others in the years to come.

> *Taste and see that the Lord is good!*

CHAPTER 23
BUT WAIT . . . THERE'S MORE!

Some people dream of retirement as a time to do nothing but relax. Yet, Conlee and I can't find anything in the Bible about retirement. After over twenty years as a professional engineer, and then twenty years as the pastor of a church, Conlee "retired" from his position. Yet, we both prefer to describe this next season of our lives as a "re-assignment."

We have never been busier, yet it is a great kind of busy-ness. We are able to follow opportunities that God offers us without the responsibilities and pressures of the demands of a job. We are ministering, playing, loving, laughing, and finding a new kind of rest that is productive. We listen to God more and are eager to do new things with His direction. He has opened up opportunities we never dreamed possible.

Although we had some rocking chairs on the porch, they are now in the storeroom. We don't have time to sit and rock. There are just too many interesting things to do!

If you are not facing an important change in your life right now, you will at some point. You may marry, have children, move with your work, become an empty-nester, lose a loved one, have grandchildren, become ill, or retire. All of these life changes are very high on the Holmes and Rahe Stress Scale.[69] Although some of them are positive and some are negative, each one can cause stress and perhaps illness as the stress affects the physical body. Is this God's plan for us to have increased stress each time we experience changes in our life routines? I think not!

God's plan is to experience each life change in intimate relationship with Him! We receive His perspective instead of the world's. We receive His strength instead of relying on our own. We are empowered by Him much more than by Social Security, insurance policies or pension plans.

Do you still have that picture of the toddler we started off with? It's never too late to live into that picture. God delights in keeping us eternally young.

I hope that by now you are experiencing some things you may not have thought about when you began this book.

- God speaks to His people today. He speaks to you! He delights in conversations with you.
- You can hear God! You are spiritually and physically equipped to hear His voice in any manner He chooses to speak to you.
- Hearing what He says to you in intimate, personal ways will change you little by little into the person He created you to be.

---

69   Psychiatrists Thomas Holmes and Richard Rahe examined the medical records of over 5,000 medical patients in 1967, to determine whether stressful events might cause illnesses. Patients were asked to tally a list of 43 life events based on a relative score. A definite correlation was found between their life events and their illnesses.

- Taking seriously the words He speaks to you will change the ways you relate to others and to your environment.
- God has exciting new experiences for you every day! Just ask Him to show you what they are.
- The changes God makes in you will change the world for His purposes. That means your friends, your family, your children's children, and their children.

The results of your conversations with God will range from elementary truths to concepts that at first might seem to be rather grandiose. *Can God really use me to change the world?* Yes, of course He can. And He will!

Think about what has happened to you since you made conversations with God a priority in your life.

> *Has He surprised you?*
> *Have you found a new intimacy in your*
> *relationship with Him?*
> *Has the Bible come alive for you?*
> *Have you learned more about His character?*
> *Have you experienced moments of entering into*
> *God's DIVINE TIME ZONE?*
> *Have you seen difficult people in a new light?*

I hope you realize that what once seemed like a fantasy, can now become a reality. Those of you who have been waiting for your "happily ever after" with God can actually begin to live it today! I have a sign in my office that reads:

It's Never Too Late To Live Happily Ever After!

How exciting to realize that at any moment of life you can begin this awesome journey of an intimate, vibrant, dialogical relationship with God! It may be after many false starts and stops, long lapses into forgetfulness, or turning away from God for all sorts of reasons. But, He is waiting for you today. What will He say to you as soon as you join Him? Don't miss it!

APPENDIX

Chapter Discussion Ideas

For Private Devotions with God or for Small Groups

These discussion questions would best be used in conjunction with your Listening Prayer Journal. They are organized by the chapters of the book, but not necessarily meant to be completed within a certain time frame. These reflection questions are best done leisurely, letting God keep you with each one as long as He wants to. You will receive the most benefit if you do more than just read them. Actively engage in writing out the questions and/or discussing them with a small group! There are some fill-in-the-blanks sections preceded by this symbol: ▶, all taken from the text of the book or from scripture. Have fun!

CHAPTER 1
THE ART OF CONVERSATION

1. Just as you have a designated place for sleeping and one for eating, consider making a designated place in your home where you can enter into a quiet place with Him. Where is the

most comfortable place for you to get into the "listening tent" with God like Moses did? What do you consider necessary to have with you to enhance your time with Him? Get a basket, tray, box, or pouch to keep your necessaries intact, ready to use each day. Possible items: Bible, Journal, pens, devotional book, bookmark, concordance. . .

2. Do you know anyone who quotes God as if he had a direct line to Him? How comfortable are you with this?

3. Have you ever "heard" God speak? How many times?
    Once _____ Several times _____ Occasionally _____
    Regularly _____ Never _____ Not sure _____

4. If you have heard God, how did He speak?
    Audibly? _____ Impression? _____ Images? _____
    Through others? _____ Other ways? _____

5. What did He say? _____
    _____

6. If you seldom or never hear God, would you like to? What do you think is your biggest hindrance?

7. ▶ *The two equal components of good conversation are*
    _____ *and* _____ .

8. ▶ *Participants in genuine conversation share* _____
    _____ .

9. ▶ *The fruit of genuine conversation is when participants move into an* _____

_____

_____

10. How would you evaluate the depth of genuine conversation in your family of origin?

11. Who was your primary dialogue partner when you were a child?

12. Who is your primary dialogue partner today?

13. What is your biggest obstacle to achieving meaningful conversations with others?

14. What is your biggest obstacle to achieving meaningful conversations with God?

Ask God to open your heart to desire to hear Him more frequently and with more clarity.

CHAPTER 2
PRIORITIES AND PROBLEMS

1. ▶ Write out my simple little 3-line prayer:
Lord Jesus, _____ *to my heart.*
_____ *my life.*
And make me _____. *Amen.*

2. Now, pray it aloud three times, each time putting emphasis on a different line.

3. Ask God to give you a memory of a time He spoke to your heart. Write it in your Journal or share it with others in your group.

4. Who is the little child you would choose to use as a model for the picture of awe, wonder, discovery and excitement about exploring God's world? Describe the child with some examples of his/her behavior that is endearing to you.

5. Name 5 qualities of child-like wonder that God wants you to have in your life

a. _____

b. _____

c. _____

d. _____

e. _____

Ask God to free these qualities in you so that you can more easily explore His wonders.

CHAPTER 3
OBSTACLES

1. *You're Not in the Garden Anymore* - Name several things Adam and Eve could enjoy in the Garden that you are not able to do without much effort and supernatural anointing.

a. _____

b. _____

c. _____

d. _____

e. _____

2. Name 5 things most churches expect Christians to do every
    day.

a. _____

b. _____

c. _____

d. _____

e. _____

3. List the primary goals on your typical daily routine of things
    you expect to accomplish, whether you do them or not.

a. _____

b. _____

c. _____

d. _____

e. _____

f. _____

g. _____

h. _____

4. ▶ *Sometimes you have to say* _____ *to some really*
    good things in order to say _____ *to the very best.*

5. *Crossing Off Items on Your To-Do List* - Which of the items
    from the lists above do you really love to do? _____

    _____

6. Which ones are obligatory chores? _____

   _____

7. Which ones do you put off indefinitely? _____

   _____

8. Where is your relationship with God in your list? _____

   _____

9. Ask the Lord to show you how to put Him in your daily agenda without making Him an obligation. Write what He says in your Listening Prayer Journal.

10. ▶ *Paralyzing Passivity* – The definition from Noah Webster's *1828 American Dictionary of the English Language*:
    PASSIVITY: *"The tendency of a body to*
    _____ *in a given state, either*
    of _____ *or* _____, *till*
    _____ *by another body."*

11. Give an example of passivity in the form of motion: _____

    _____

12. Give an example of passivity in the form of rest: _____

    _____

13. *That's Not My Gift* – Have you ever said or believed that you are not equipped to hear God like others do? _____

14. ▶ John 8:47: *"He who belongs to God _____ what God says. The _____ you do not _____ is that you do not _____ to God."*

15. *The Deception Dilemma* – In what areas of your life have you been deceived? _____

_____

16. In what areas of your life are you <u>fearful</u> of being deceived?

_____

17. Picture Jesus before you and hand Him the fears and the actual deceptions from your past. See what He does with what you give Him. Let Him show you how to forgive those who deceived you so that you will not be bound by their sin any longer.

18. *I'm Scared* – What is the worst thing you can imagine God saying to you? _____ Write it out in your Listening Prayer Journal and ask Him about it. Then write what He really is saying to you and when you hear His truth, cross out the fearful words that had lodged in your heart. Give them to Him as you mark through them.

19. What was your childhood image of God? _____

_____

20. What is your image of Him today? _____

_____

21. *Past the Expiration Date* – Have you ever been influenced by a dispensationalist(s) who believed that God speaking personally to His people and performing miracles was a dispensation that ended with the apostles? _____

_____

22. If so, stop right now and thank God for whatever was true that was imparted to you by this person(s) and ask Him to sort out what was in error. Many of the wrong teachings (heresy) we receive have an element of Biblical truth attached. We must be careful not to "throw out the baby with the bath water." Ask God to bind His truth to your heart in new and exciting ways, showing you in scripture, and confirming with experience.

23. Did you begin a God Month where you assume the spiritual posture of a little child? If so, write out some of your impressions of this experience. If not, begin now!

CHAPTER 4
PRIORITIES AND PRACTICE

1. What is a discipline you spent time learning and practicing? (sports, arts, lessons, etc.) _____ Did you love it or hate it? _____
Why? _____
Are you still doing it today?_____
Why? _____

2. How was a relationship with Jesus introduced into your life?

   _____

3. Name 3 ways you have intentionally and consistently maintained this relationship.

   a. _____

   b. _____

   c. _____

4. What does your typical daily routine look like?

Before breakfast _____

_____

Before noon _____

_____

Before supper _____

_____

Before bedtime _____

_____

Are any of these activities optional? Could any of them be omitted for listening time with God?

5. Have you specifically asked Holy Spirit to help you organize your schedule to make time for listening to God? _____Have you asked Him specifically to help you hear better in a way you can understand? _____ Have you asked Him to fill you with His presence more each day? _____

6. If you have not already done so, ask Him now. Then write brief impressions of what He gives you.

   _____

   _____

7. Do you have a listening prayer partner? _____ Have you ever had one? _____ What are the best qualities of having someone listen with you? _____

   _____

   What are the most difficult? _____

   _____

You can evaluate your answers either on past or present experiences or your desires for the future.

8. When you go into the "tent" with the Lord, do you let Him set the agenda? _____ What has He initiated recently that surprised you? _____

   _____

CHAPTER 5
LISTENING 101

1. ▶ *Deuteronomy 30: 11, 14 – "What I am commanding you today is ____ ____ _____ for you or _____ _____ _____ . . . The word is very ____ ___; it is in your _____ and in your _____ so you may _____ it."*

2. Ask God to lead you to a scripture of His choosing. Though it

may seem tedious at first, go through the following steps to experience the rhythm of listening prayer:

    a. First, read it silently.

    b. Then, read it aloud.

    c. Then, listen to God speak it to you.

    d. Let it marinate a moment inside your soul.

    e. Then ask God to clarify, amplify, or personalize it to you.

    f. Write what He gives you in your Listening Prayer Journal.

3. Looking at what you wrote in your Journal after listening to God, answer the following questions:

    a. Does this line up with scripture?

    b. Does it build me up or tear me down? Does it accuse me or affirm me?

    c. Does it bring me closer to God?

    d. What difference will it make in my life?

CHAPTER 6
THE ULTIMATE, END-ALL, FINAL, DECISIVE, DEFINITIVE, VITAL, REFERENCE BOOK

1. Try to remember all the Bible studies you have done. Which ones were strictly informational? _____

_____

_____

Which ones were inspiring and brought you closer to God?

_____

Which ones were boring? _____

Which were too difficult? _____

Which was the most challenging? _____

_____

2. How did you choose these studies? _____

_____

3. Have you ever asked God to find you a Bible study that He knows is suitable for you? If you do ask Him, keep your eyes and ears open so you won't miss it! It may come unexpectedly, or in an unusual setting.

CHAPTER 7
A LISTENING PRAYER JOURNAL

1. Write your definition of dialogue. Who is involved? What are the characteristics of good dialogue? What is its purpose?

_____

_____

2. ▶ Hebrew verb review from Exodus 2:23-25. Give an expanded definition:

   a. *Shema* means _____

_____

   b. *Zakhor* means _____

_____

   c. *Yada* means _____

_____

3. How do these Hebrew verbs describe listening prayer?

   _____

   _____

4. How would you describe our Human Time Zone (HTZ) / *Chronos?* _____

   _____

5. How would you describe God's Divine Time Zone (DTZ) / *Kairos?* _____

   _____

6. ▶ The literal translation of the Greek word *kairos* is: the

   _____.

7. Think of an example from your life when answered prayer from God came after a long time of believing He did not hear or did not care. _____

   _____

8. What are the circumstances that had to fall in place for His answer to come to pass? _____

9. In your Listening Prayer Journal, begin to write without questioning Him, what God says to you about "Who I Am in Christ." If your doubts about hearing Him correctly include *I just wanted to hear that,* be assured that He put that desire in your heart.

CHAPTER 8
LEARNING A NEW LANGUAGE

1. What are some characteristics of the Language of the Heart?
    _____

2. How did Jesus first call you to belong to Him?
    Was it by a "warming of the heart?" _____
    Circumstances? _____
    A logical decision? _____
    Supernatural visitation? _____
    Emotional response? _____
    Other? _____

3. Was the initial way He spoke to your heart the way you expect
    every day? How do you expect Him to speak to you? _____
    _____
    _____

4. ▶ *Intellect + Emotional Experience =*_____
    Give a personal example of this spiritual equation:
    _____
    _____

5. How does a Biblical definition of reason differ from a worldly
    definition? _____

6. Where do you place yourself on this spectrum when typically making a "reasonable" decision?

Intellect/Logic....................*Reason*...................*Emotion/Feelings*
COGNITIVE   **HEART**   **INTUITIVE**

7. How was Art Katz looking for truth before he boarded the Greek ship? _____

8. How did Jesus speak to him? _____
_____

9. What event in the life of Jesus speaks to your heart in a deeply personal way? _____
_____
_____

CHAPTER 9
ONE GOD WHO SPEAKS IN MANY WAYS
In an Audible Voice and Through The Bible

1. List as many examples as you can of people hearing God speak in an audible voice, biblically and in modern times. _____
_____
_____

2. What is a common denominator with the examples? _____
_____

3. If you have seldom (or never) asked God to give you a passion for His Word, make yourself reminders to do this for a week and experience the hunger He places within you. He loves to answer this prayer!

4. Experiment with some new ways of approaching the Word of God such as some of the following examples. Check the ones that are new to you.

   _____ Read until God highlights a passage

   _____ Write out a passage substituting your name and personal pronouns

   _____ Write out each command from Jesus, making them personal

   _____ Read only the red letter words

   _____ Improvise a scene from the Gospels in your imagination, putting yourself in the story and/or identifying with one of the characters

   _____ Others

5. Go back to #4 and circle the ones you want to try.

CHAPTER 10
ONE GOD WHO SPEAKS IN MANY WAYS
Through Dreams, Sermons, Teachings, and Books

1. Do you have a recurrent dream? Write it out in your Listening Prayer Journal and ask God about it.

2. Ask Him to give you meaningful dreams and help you to remember them.

3. What are your expectations of sermons? _____
   _____

4. How can you tell if a preacher has heard from God in his sermon, or if he is repeating what he heard or read from someone else? _____
   _____

5. How often do you pray for your pastor to have an enlarged capacity to hear God? _____

6. What do you do with a sermon after you hear it? _____
   _____

7. What kind of teacher (or who) inspires you to come closer to God? _____

8. What author challenges you to come closer to God? _____
   _____

9. If you don't already do so, begin to take notes of important ideas from good books. Keep them in your Listening Prayer Journal for references in your conversations with God.

CHAPTER 11
ONE GOD WHO SPEAKS IN MANY WAYS
Through Worship

1. What is your definition of worship? _____
    _____

2. What is the Bible's definition? *(Use your concordance and get
    a comprehensive view)* _____
    _____

3. Worship is very personal because it brings you into the heart
    of God. Not every form of corporate worship can do this for
    everyone. However, when many people are worshiping freely
    together, you can be transported into His presence, even if it
    is not your favorite way. Can you give some personal exam-
    ples of this? _____
    _____

4. What manner of corporate worship draws you closest to God?
    _____

5. What manner of private worship draws you closest to God?
    _____

6. Explain *horizontal* worship: _____
    _____

7. Explain *vertical* worship: _____
    _____

8. ▶ Ruth Ward Heflin: "_____ *until the Spirit of* _____ *comes.* _____ *until the* _____ *comes. Then,* _____ *in the* _____."

9. Is there a progression to worship? How would you explain it?

   _____

10. What is the primary component in true vertical worship? ____

    _____

11. Ask Jesus to send you His Spirit of worship!

CHAPTER 12
ONE GOD WHO SPEAKS IN MANY WAYS
Through Prophecy

1. Write a definition of *THE CALLING OF A PROPHET*: _____

   _____

2. Write a definition of *THE GIFT OF PROPHECY* _____

   _____

3. Who is your favorite prophet in the Bible? _____

   _____

   Why? _____

4. Do you know someone today with the calling of a prophet on his/her life? _____

Describe both the honor and the criticism this person receives.

_____

5. ▶ 1 Corinthians 14:1 – *"Follow the way of _____ and _____ _____ spiritual gifts, especially the gift of _____."*

6. How has God used you to exercise the gift of prophecy? _____
_____

7. Do you *eagerly* desire to be used in this way? _____

8. Have you ever given someone a word from God (using the gift of prophecy) and been rejected? _____

9. What effect did this have on your desire to live a prophetic life? _____

10. Have you been the recipient of a prophecy? _____
What was the fruit? _____
Did it bring you closer to God? _____
Did it glorify Jesus or did it exalt the prophet? _____
Are you still waiting to understand it? _____

11. Write out 1 John 4:1-3a. Use this standard to test the prophetic. _____

12. Write out any prophecies you have been given as the Lord reminds you of them. Ask Him questions and listen to what He says to you. Write it all in your Journal.

CHAPTER 13
ONE GOD WHO SPEAKS MANY WAYS
Through Holy Silence and Through Impressions

1. When you are alone, do you automatically turn on music, TV, or radio? _____ Explain why.

2. Stop right now and jot down all the background noises that are present with you, listening carefully to become aware of those you tune out. _____

   _____

3. Ask God to show you any reasons why you might avoid (or be afraid of) silence.

4. I was told once to picture myself sitting in God's lap, absolutely quiet, relaxing my mind and body into His presence. Then, to be aware of which of us moves first. Try it!

5. As you read the section on "Impressions," what person or event came to your mind? _____

6. Ask God to give you a new awareness of the many subtle impressions you receive during the day. Write them out in your Listening Prayer Journal and see if this is another creative way in which He speaks to your heart.

CHAPTER 14
IMAGINE THAT!

1. ▶ The Hebrew word translated "imagination" in the Bible is *yetzer* which means _____.

2. ▶ 1 Chronicles 29:18, KJV: *O Lord God of* _____, _____, *and* _____, *our fathers, keep this forever in the* _____ *(yetzer) of the* _____ *of the* _____ *of Your people, and direct their* _____ *unto You.*

3. What determines the content of one's imagination? _____
   _____

4. What are some ways in which you purposefully fill your imagination? _____

5. What are some involuntary ways in which your imagination is filled? _____

6. Which of the testimonies about "Changing the Leopard's Spots" speaks most to your heart? Explain why or write it in your Journal. _____
   _____

7. If you have never done so before, take some time to ask God to cleanse your imagination. This is something we all need to do on a regular basis. It is always surprising to discover what He reveals.

CHAPTER 15
QUESTIONING GOD

1. Without judging, list 5 Christian traditions you typically accept without question. (These are not Biblical admonitions, but parts of the Christian faith you have accepted as the norm in your life).

a. _____

b. _____

c. _____

d._____

e._____

2. Again, without judging, list 5 traditions other Christians typically accept that you have never tried.

a. _____

b. _____

c. _____

d. _____

e. _____

3. ▶ Write out Hebrews 5:14 - _____

_____

4. ▶ In contrast to solid food for mature Christians, list the 6 teachings that Paul identifies as elementary for the church (Hebrew 6:1-2):

a. _____

b. _____

c. _____

d. _____

e. _____

f. _____

5. What is the desire of your heart? _____

_____

Enjoy a conversation with God about your desires!

CHAPTER 16
YOU HAVE THE WRONG NUMBER

1. When you are born again you are equipped by Holy Spirit to
    be used in any of the 9 gifts listed in 1 Corinthians 12:8-10.
    List them below with a short description of how God has used
    you with each one. If you have not experienced any of them
    yet, would you be willing?

a._____

b._____

c._____

d._____

e._____

f._____

g._____

h._____

i._____

2. Why is the discerning of spirits vital to all the other gifts? ___
   _____

3. When a telemarketer calls you, how do you typically respond?
   _____

4. How does this response compare to your responses to the lures of the world, flesh and the devil?

CHAPTER 17
THE AUTHENTIC VOICE OF THE SHEPHERD

1. ▶ Deuteronomy 30:19b-20 – *"Now _____ _____, so that you and your children may _____ and that you may _____ the Lord your God, _____ to His voice, and _____ _____ to Him. For the Lord is your _____, and He will give you many _____ in the land He swore to give to your fathers, Abraham, Isaac and Jacob."*

2. What are some of the things you learned about sheep and shepherds when reading this chapter?
   _____
   _____
   _____
   _____

3. How does each characteristic describe the relationship Jesus, the Good Shepherd, has with us?
   _____

_____

_____

_____

4. Write out John 10:26-28: _____

_____

CHAPTER 18
THE COUNTERFEITS
The World

1. ▶ The two primary characteristics of those who find their comfort and identity in the world are:

_____

2. What does the world say to you about:

a. your money _____

_____

b. your security _____

_____

c. your free time _____

_____

d. your life goals _____

_____

e. your friends _____

_____

f. your children _____

_____

g. your sexuality _____

h. your death _____

_____

3. How have these values changed in your lifetime?

_____

4. What does the Word of God say to you about the same subjects?

a. 1 Tim 6:10, Matt 6:24 _____

_____

b. Psa 125:1, John 10:28, Heb 13:6 _____

_____

c. Eph 5:15-16, Psa 90:12 _____

_____

d. John 12:25, Psa 37, Prov 3:5 _____

_____

e. Prov 17:17, Eccles 4:4-10, John 15:13 _____

_____

f. 1 Tim 3:4, Eph 6:1, Matt 11:25 _____

_____

g. 1 Thess 4:3-5, 1 Cor 6:18-20 _____

_____

h. 2 Tim 1:10, John 11:25,26 _____

_____

CHAPTER 19
THE COUNTERFEITS
The Flesh

1. One definition of "flesh" is used in Galatians 5:24-25. This refers to crucifying (putting to death) one's sinful nature. Write out this scripture, personalizing it to make it your own declaration: _____

    _____

2. How would you define another way "flesh" is used in Ezekiel 36:26? _____

    _____

3. How is "flesh" defined in John 1:14? _____

    _____

4. In dealing with the need to both *renounce the sins of the flesh* and to also *get to the root of the problem*, I used the example of a leaky ceiling and the stains left behind. What example is meaningful to you? _____

    _____

5. How would you react if Jesus told you to "kill" something in your life? How would you do it?

6. How does this relate to Jesus' words in Matthew 18:8-9? ___

    _____

CHAPTER 20
THE COUNTERFEITS
The Devil

1. Have you ever been in a group that spent time in prayer making declarations to the devil?

   _____

2. How effective were their prayers? _____

   _____

3. What are the dangers in such a practice? _____

   _____

4. ▶ Biblically, *Satan* means: "an _____, a _____, or an _____."

5. What are the characteristics of accusation?

   _____

6. What are the characteristics of Godly conviction?

   _____

7. Can you describe a situation where you were accused of doing something? What were your reactions? How did you continue to feel about your accuser?

   _____

   _____

   _____

   _____

8. What are the characteristics of slander?

    _____

9. Have you ever been slandered? _____
    If so, what was the result? _____
    Did the slanderous words wound your character or your
    pride? _____

10. What is the ultimate goal of a real adversary?

    _____

11. Which tactic of the devil are you most susceptible to:
    deception, seduction, or *intimidation?*

    _____

    Give examples: _____

    _____

12. In conversation with God, affirm that you are secure in the
    3 antidotes to the influences of the world, flesh and the
    devil.

a. Do I <u>really</u> know that Jesus is Lord? Is it the kind of
    knowing that comes from a love relationship and bears
    fruit? Do I experience the full benefits of that relationship?

b. Am I empowered by Holy Spirit? Am I letting Him guide
    my prayers? Am I protected by His armor? Do I frequently
    ask Him for more power in my life?

c.   Am I willing to renounce any influences the Lord show me that draw me away from Him and His purposes for my life?

CHAPTER 21
PAST TENSE – FUTURE PERFECT

1.   How have your earthly father and mother defined you? Do any words or lack of words from them ring in your thoughts?

_____

_____

2.   Did you have childhood nicknames? _____
How did they make you feel? _____

_____

3.   What was your family motto (spoken or unspoken)? _____

_____

_____

4.   When you think of the most painful/embarrassing moment of your life, what comes to mind?

_____

_____

_____

5.   Have you ever submitted this event to the Lord and asked Him to redefine it for you? _____

6. Could you write out now what Jesus says to you about it, and/or share it with prayer partners?

7. How does the idea of having a listening prayer partner seem to you? _____ Is it appealing? _____
    Frightening? _____ Not sure? _____

8. What would be important for you to trust a listening prayer partner? _____

9. In Chapter 15 I asked you to write out the desire of your heart. What was it then? _____
    What is it today? _____

10. Would you be willing to give your desire to Jesus? If so, be sure to see what He does with it, what He says to you about it, and what He places back into your heart.

    _____

11. What motto is the Lord giving you and your family?

    _____

If you're not sure, ask Him for one!

CHAPTER 22
A MATTER OF TASTE

1. Write out Psalm 119:103 - _____

_____

2. Can you think of an example when God asked you to do something you believed would be unpleasant or extremely difficult? _____

_____

3. If you yielded to Him, how did it turn out? _____

_____

4. If you are in the midst of such an experience, does this give you hope? _____

CHAPTER 23
BUT WAIT . . . THERE'S MORE!

1. Do you still have the picture of your toddler inspiration?

_____

2. Keeping in mind the God-given capacities to be child-like in His Kingdom, what are some of the characteristics you have begun to experience? _____

_____

_____

3. How do you respond to the statement: *God will use you to change the world!*

_____

_____

RESOURCES

- **The Journey to Wholeness in Christ** conferences
- **S✝EPS** weekends
- ***The Journey to Wholeness in Christ*** devotional book by Signa Bodishbaugh
- ***Illusions of Intimacy*** by Signa Bodishbaugh
- **"Journey Groups"** DVD Small Group Studies with workbooks and leader's guide with Conlee and Signa Bodishbaugh
- ***The Journey to Wholeness in Christ*** 12 CD album of conference, recorded live, with Conlee and Signa Bodishbaugh
- **When God Speaks . . .** 7 CD album of Torah Studies with Signa Bodishbaugh
- **Heaven the City of God** CD for those who are grieving or dying, with Signa Bodishbaugh, music by Kirk Dearman
- **Holy Spirit** CD, with Signa Bodishbaugh

All information about conferences and ordering products are found on our website: www.JTWIC.org

FaceBook: *The Journey to Wholeness in Christ*

Special Thanks

There have been so many people who have supported me while writing this book. It first began many, many years ago when teaching a series of classes called, "How to Hear God's Voice in a Loud and Noisy World." The response was amazing and I realized that most people only need a little encouragement to begin to listen to God and actually hear what He is saying to them. The men and women in that class were so excited that some of them would send me long pages copied from their Listening Prayer Journals of what He was saying to them.

Whenever we are invited to speak somewhere the organizers always want to make sure that we cover the subject of hearing God. It seems that many Christians think it is going to be really difficult to hear Him, and daunting to initiate a time to do so. But there is a hunger in their hearts to experience meaningful conversations with Him. And, when they do, it's transforming!

When I started writing this book the form was much more like I was teaching that class. One of the best things said to me was from my good friend, Joy Hilley. Joy is also a writer, an editor, and a very honest and loving person. About two years ago we met for coffee on New Year's Eve morning at Panera Bread and she said, "Your material is good, and it's factual. But parts of it are 'ho-hum.' You are not a 'ho-hum' person. You have to put yourself into it." She and her husband, Joe, both wonderfully "no-nonsense" people, have been great cheerleaders for me.

Then I was contacted by a developmental editor from Nav-Press who, after much discussion, decided I was not a good match for their current project, but gave me some excellent advice. "Decide who you are speaking to in your book. Give that person a profile. Talk to that one person and make it personal."

So, the original manuscript was tossed, and I re-wrote the book as a conversation with one person. The person I chose to "see" across from my desk may surprise you. I named him "Coach," and he is a middle-aged Christian man who is definitely not feely-touchy or overly sentimental. He has a great sense of humor. He's a "by the Book" kind of guy but doesn't hear personally from God very well or even expect to. He's very moral and well-liked, but seldom talks about anything too personal. He is not a real person but he is modeled on one of my son's friends, a man I have never actually met. I imagined questions and responses from Coach, and I wanted to make sure he understood everything I wrote. So, "Coach, this book is for you!" And it's for all the Coach-es out there who never thought they needed to hear or could hear God's voice.

Judy Oschwald has read various forms of this manuscript, made corrections, and encouraged and prayed for me all along. She is a prime example of being a good friend and a listening prayer partner.

And very special thanks to Conlee, who has lovingly allowed me to slip from his warm embrace every morning at 3:30 or 4:00 to go to my tent and write out what God speaks to me.

And even more lovingly, he has blessed me when I'm ready to go to bed when it gets dark. He has read, re-read, and re-re-read what I write and always calls me to "say it better," or "put it in your conversational voice." He has great instincts for what will minister to God's people and he has loved me unconditionally and patiently. And he is still my #1 listening prayer partner.

And, thank You, Lord, for taking me into Your tent and speaking to my heart, changing my life, and making me whole!

Signa Bodishbaugh
Hamewith Cottage

You have a story.
We want to publish it.

Everyone has as a story to tell. It might be about something you know how to do, or what has happened in your life, or it may be a thrilling, or romantic, or intriguing, or heart-warming, or suspenseful story, starring a cast of characters that have been swimming around in your imagination.

And at Wyatt House Publishing, we can get your story onto the pages of a book just like the one you are holding in your hand. With professional interior design and a custom, professionally designed cover built just for you from the start, you can finally see your dream of being an author become reality. Then, you will see your book listed with retailers all over the world as people are able to buy your book from wherever they are and have it delivered to their home or their e-reader.

So what are you waiting for? This is your time.

CPSIA information can be obtained at www.ICGtesting.com
Printed in the USA
LVOW05s0758230114

370648LV00007B/63/P